W9-BMY-351

Navigating a Life

Henry W. Bloch

John Hare

Navigating a Life

Henry Bloch in World War II

by John Herron and
Mary Ann Wynkoop

BkMk Press
University of Missouri-Kansas City
www.umkc.edu/bkmk

BkMk Press
University of Missouri-Kansas City
5101 Rockhill Road
Kansas City, Missouri 64110
www.umkc.edu/bkmk

Executive editor: Robert Stewart
Managing editor: Ben Furnish
Assistant managing editor: Cynthia Beard

Library of Congress Cataloging-in-Publication Data available.

ISBN 978-0-933532-18-2

Acknowledgments

Getting to know Henry Bloch—even a little bit—for this project was incredibly rewarding. Each time we met, usually in his fifth-floor office near the Country Club Plaza, we would follow the same routine. I would start with a single question about the war and then prepare to take notes, as Henry recounted his experiences. I would occasionally interrupt to clarify a detail or ask a follow up question, but for the most part, I listened. I did so because when he spoke, stories that were more than seven decades old came back in vivid detail. Whether Henry brought me to the training grounds of Texas, the airfields of England, or the skies over Germany, he was as passionate as he was so long ago as a young army officer.

As readers will discover in the pages that follow, however, such engagement and excitement rarely led to bravado. Henry was (and is) modest when describing his achievements. He graduated from the University of Michigan, even though, as he would have you believe, he was a second-rate student; he survived the war only because of dumb luck; or, my favorite, his homespun, family accounting business thrived because of the contributions of others. Those in this community who have known Henry Bloch for far longer than I are well familiar with such self-deprecation, but for me, encountering him for the first time, it was humbling. It did, however, put the war and its influence on Henry in context. Henry's wartime experiences, and how he remembers them, prove that in many ways, the Second World War was the event of his life. How the war cuts through his career is the subject of this small volume.

Telling this story required the help of many people. A graduate student in the History Department at the University of Missouri-Kansas City, Matthew Reeves, served as the project's senior research associate and conducted the first oral interviews with Henry. Matthew also organized the Bloch family papers and helped with many of the photographs that appear in this book. Dr. Mary Ann Wynkoop, UMKC American Studies professor emerita, also contributed to the success of this book. She researched key aspects of Henry's life, investigated the policies and protocols of the Army Air Corps, and produced working drafts of several chapters. David Miles, head of the Marion and Henry Bloch Family Foundation, was instrumental in keeping this book project on track and moving forward, as was Tom Bloch. Indeed, it was Tom's original idea—to produce "a legacy gift for the grandkids"—that provided the original impetus for this book. David Disney, a Bloch family friend and senior vice president at J.E. Dunn, tracked down Henry's mission records from the National Archives and Records Administration. These sources provided key details about Henry's time in the European theater. Other information about Henry's war experiences came from Michael Darter and Gerald Grove of the 95th Bomb Group (H) Memorials Foundation. I was fortunate that Henry's unit, the Ninety-Fifth, has been the subject of considerable historical interest. Of special note is the work of Rob Morris and Ian Hawkins. I encourage readers who want to learn more about the flight operations of the Eighth Air Force to consult the work of these two prominent military scholars. Two additional authors deserve special mention. John A. Byrne's *Whiz Kids* is an incredibly helpful resource for readers interested in the army's Statistical Control program. I am also much indebted to Thomas M. Bloch's *Many Happy Returns*, the best available book on Henry's life and legacy.

Finally, a sincere thank you to Henry Wollman Bloch who made working on this book project very enjoyable.

—John Herron

Contents

Foreword

This book is about the American spirit, embodied in the men and women who fought in World War II. Henry Bloch, through his early life and his decision to join the fight for freedom, especially exemplifies this spirit. In the process we learn not only about Henry, but we also get extraordinary insight into those who fought for liberty alongside him and faced their own mortality just as he did. Through Henry, we also learn the remarkable impact these brave men and women had on the past seventy years of American history.

During college at the University of Michigan, Henry was swept up by the war that was then spreading around the world. He had one driving thought—to serve his country. He chose to join the Army Air Corps. That one decision would also put him on a path toward the most dangerous military specialty during all of the war, regardless of the war-time theater—as a B-17 crewmember in the Eighth Air Force flying over Germany and other European countries.

Henry liked his military training, and he excelled at it. He liked the discipline and work ethic. Among other benefits, he got to meet and train with a cross section of America, no doubt eye opening for this product of the Midwest. By the time he learned that he was going to England, it was no secret that the Mighty Eighth had sustained horrific losses attacking German industrial capability. Despite the grim outlook for Allied forces, he remained optimistic and never wavered about his ability to have an impact on the conflict.

In a glimpse into the kind of son he was, in deference to his mother, he agreed not to be a pilot, since she saw it as too dangerous. He became a navigator instead. What he understood, but his mother did not, was that as part of a ten-man crew inside the aluminum B-17 bomber, all shared the danger equally, irrespective of their duties, whether in front, in back, or on the top or bottom.

His introduction to his wartime base in Horham, England, a small Suffolk village in East Anglia, was shocking. When Henry was given the bunk of a man who didn't return from that day's mission, he took it in stride. He was now a member of the Ninety-Fifth Bomb Group, part of the Eighth Air Force. It was here he would carry out the new strategy introduced in WWII to use air power to deplete the enemy's capacity to wage war. His first mission was an extremely tough one, and he said that was the one mission where he thought he deserved a medal. As you read further, I predict you will conclude that there were many other missions where he also deserved recognition.

But Henry Bloch wasn't about medals. Henry was about serving his country. Serving his country meant he had to summon his courage every time he strapped into his B-17. He defied the odds and completed thirty-two missions. "I wasn't a hero, just doing my job," as he would later say. He accepted his duties in the air, stoically thinking, *if I die, I die.* I'm sure this was a thought many of his fellow warriors had as well, no matter whether on the ground, in the air, or at sea. Henry overcame his fear and compiled an impressive wartime record.

Henry Bloch came back to America a changed man. He was still the optimistic, intellectually curious, and persistent person he was when he left. But his military experience left him fundamentally changed in ways that would continue to bless America. Henry was no longer afraid; he was not afraid to fail and was no longer self-limiting in what he would attempt. WWII forever altered his views of risk taking. As the book makes clear, there would be no H&R Block without his experiences in military training and combat above the European continent.

Henry's story is unique but gives us insight into why we call this the *Greatest Generation.* They not only risked their lives to make the world free again; they often took great risks to make America great once they returned from the fields of battle. Like Henry, this generation never lost their humanity or their optimism. Americans will forever be indebted to Henry Bloch and those he represents. He may not call himself a hero, but I do.

Richard B. Myers
General, USAF, Ret.
Fifteenth Chairman of the Joint Chiefs of Staff

A Note from the Bloch Family

Our father's life has been a fascinating journey in at least three distinct ways. First, the creation of tax-preparation giant H&R Block was, by all accounts, a groundbreaking entrepreneurial success. Second was Dad's fervent desire to give back to his hometown through extraordinary philanthropy. This may well prove to be his greatest legacy. But this book focuses on a third part of his journey, one that took place before the other two. None of us recall hearing much about this earlier part of Dad's life, and it had not really been probed by anyone until now.

Bookshelves are filled with stories of the exploits of the United States in World War II. Countless stories have been told about such military giants as Eisenhower, Patton, and MacArthur. But few of the other sixteen million American soldiers who courageously served their country in combat during that perilous period in history are remembered as heroes. We have come to learn that Dad epitomized the spirit of those brave, unrecognized men and women who successfully rallied against the Nazi war machine.

The four of us learned in our high school history classes that World War II was the most widespread war ever waged. More than one hundred million people from thirty countries were involved. We also learned that the conflict was the deadliest war in global history, with over fifty million civilians and military personnel killed. Included in this staggering total were six million Jews executed in concentration camps. Among the millions of Americans who served in the armed forces during the war, more than four hundred thousand died.

Little did our parents, both Jewish, and the millions of other teenagers who grew up in the United States during the 1930s know that the chancellor of Germany had ambitions for world domination. A decade later, when our father was in his junior year in college, it became apparent that Adolf Hitler's aggression would not only disrupt political and economic stability but would also vastly alter the trajectory of Dad's life.

In this book's introduction, General Myers aptly refers to the *Greatest Generation*, a term Tom Brokaw used in his 1988 book of the same title to describe the men and women who grew up during the Great Depression and then participated in the war effort. Brokaw suggests that this generation did not seek fame but rather saw volunteering for the war as simply *the right thing to do.* Today, as the number of people who can give first-hand accounts from World War II continues to decline, fewer Americans are able to recall stories about family members from that generation, including the turmoil they experienced and the enduring contributions they made.

Like millions of other young men at the time, our father answered his nation's call. And like many who returned from military service, he rarely uttered a word about his war experience. He understood his military experiences as his duty, a responsibility to protect his nation's freedom. Why, Dad thought, should he then brag about something that millions like him were expected to do? Fulfilling an obligation was not considered bravery or heroism.

Dad served in the Ninety-Fifth Bomb Group of the United States Army Air Force in the European theater as a navigator on a B-17, a four-engine heavy bomber. During his tour of duty, he was part of a campaign of strategic, devastating, and sometimes horrific aerial attacks on factories, railways, cities, and harbors. No amount of formal training adequately prepared him and his crew members for what they encountered on their missions. With enemy fighters and flak from anti-aircraft fire constantly aiming to tear into their formation, it is remarkable that his plane didn't blow up or break apart like many others did.

As readers will learn in the pages to follow, the war taught our father to become a fatalist. "I never knew what the next day would bring," he once told us. "But I figured I had a job to do, and I would give it my all." That same determination served him incredibly well after the war.

Immediately after his tour of duty in Europe, the Army Air Corps sent him to Harvard University for a highly selective officer-training program. He often skipped lunch on campus in favor of browsing the bookshelves of the school's library. One day he stumbled upon a pamphlet written by a Harvard professor that gave him the inspiration to start a business with his two brothers. "If it weren't for World War II," Dad reminded us, "H&R Block would never have been born."

In this book, you will get a close look at our father as an American hero. But like many heroes of the Second World War, he was extraordinarily ordinary. And like many of the Greatest Generation, he could have been described as a hardworking, selfless, and tenacious soldier. In combat, he learned how to deal with defeat and victory. Years later, he would apply his wartime lessons to life in peacetime America.

It wasn't all that unusual in the late 1940s and early 1950s for war veterans to become successful businessmen. But, against all odds, Dad became one of the greatest entrepreneurs of his generation.

Understanding his experiences in World War II is helping us, his four children, strive to achieve some measure of significance in our own lives. We hope Lieutenant Henry Bloch's war experiences might help others, including our own children and grandchildren, to do the same.

Bob Bloch
Tom Bloch
Mary Jo Brown
Liz Uhlmann

Prologue

It was late summer 1939. As he waited for his train in Kansas City's Union Station, Henry Bloch gazed out the station's ornate cathedral windows and onto the expanse of green that framed the Liberty Memorial. Built in classical Egyptian-revival style, the memorial was constructed as a testament to the sacrifice of millions during World War I. In 1921, more than two hundred thousand people, including Vice President Calvin Coolidge and the supreme military commanders from Italy, Belgium, France, Great Britain, and the United States, gathered in Kansas City for the memorial's elaborate groundbreaking ceremony. Dozens of newsreel cameras captured the event—complete with speeches, bands, parades, and the presentation of ceremonial flags to visiting dignitaries by local war veteran Harry S. Truman—for history. Almost exactly five years later, November 1926, Calvin Coolidge, now as president, returned for the dedication, explaining to the gathered crowd that the memorial had "not been raised to commemorate war and victory, but rather the results of war and victory, which are embodied in peace and liberty."

Liberty Memorial Dedication, November 11, 1926

Today, as nearly a century ago, the memorial complex is impressive. At its center stands a limestone tower jutting more than two hundred feet into the midwestern sky. From the top of the tower, visitors can gaze to the east and see Union Hill Cemetery, final resting spot for many of the region's Civil War soldiers. To the west lie the Missouri River bottoms and the city's agricultural and industrial core. Just to the north is Union Station, the railway depot that put Kansas City on the national map as a *crossroads city*. Carved on the face of the large stone obelisk are four statues—Honor, Courage, Patriotism, and Sacrifice. Each stoic figure clasps a sword and stands vigilant and dutiful. Perhaps more impressive still is that on either side of the large spire, guarding the entrance to the memorial, are two massive Assyrian sphinxes, Memory and Future. The sphinxes face one another, their expansive wings draped over their faces. Memory looks east, toward Europe, the past, and the horror that was the Great War. Future faces west, toward a more hopeful horizon, but she, too, shields her eyes, fearful of what tomorrow may bring.

As he waited for his train, Henry also had good reason to be anxious. He was leaving the cocoon of home and family to attend college more than seven hundred miles away in Michigan. But like many Americans, Henry must have felt a more distressing concern. In 1939, many citizens watched the growing expansion of fascism in Germany and beyond with great trepidation. Alarmed Americans worried that German aggression had set the stage for the unthinkable: a second world conflict. Throughout much of the decade, Adolf Hitler led Germany up from the ashes of the Weimar Republic on an expansionist path. By channeling the popular frustration with the past regime into a powerful political ideology, Hitler and his National Socialist German Workers' Party (Nazis) peddled the dream of a greater Germany that would dominate the political fortunes of Europe. In 1936, these ideas turned to action, as the rebuilt German army invaded the Rhineland, and two years later, when Henry was just sixteen, Germany annexed Austria and parts of

Czechoslovakia. An anxious world held its collective breath, hoping that the fragile peace that had held the world together since 1919 would endure.

At that moment, looking out at the Liberty Memorial, it would have been impossible for the teenage Henry not to think about the costs and consequences of World War I. When business leaders in his hometown united to build the memorial, it was a testament to the political engagement and civic spirit of this small midwestern city. Kansas City residents were rightfully proud that the Liberty Memorial, a complex built to honor the sacrifice of an entire generation lost to battle, was built in their community. Two decades earlier, young men Henry's age had fought in Europe's trenches; all too soon it would be his turn. Like all students bound for college, Henry knew that he would make choices about classes, companions, and careers that would impact the rest of his life. What he could not know, of course, was how contemporary global events would change his world forever. Unexpectedly, lessons he learned in college became preparation for an immersion in war as an Army Air Corps navigator, just as the experience of combat would, in turn, prepare him for life on a dramatic scale. That day at the station, as summer reluctantly gave way to fall, the young underclassman might already have looked forward to graduation and the opportunity to begin both family and career. Instead, he would be pulled into the great campaign to save the world from fascism. Like the paired sphinxes behind him, Henry would soon confront the challenges of war and the mystery of an unknown future.

Henry Bloch waited for the train that would start him on an improbable journey that would catapult him from a cozy college campus to the contested skies over western Europe.

Beginnings

When Henry Bloch waived goodbye to his family, gathered his belongings, and boarded the train bound for Ann Arbor, Michigan, he had no way of knowing that he was at the beginning of such an unexpected adventure. Many of his Kansas City classmates took a much shorter journey that season. Several friends from Southwest High School chose the small town of Lawrence and the nearby University of Kansas for college. Others, perhaps more loyal to the Show-Me state, took a three-hour drive in the opposite direction to the University of Missouri in Columbia. Henry could easily have made a similar choice. After all, his older brother, Leon Jr., studied in Columbia, and sibling gravity had a heavy pull on the seventeen-year-old. But Henry had a different idea—he was bound for the University of Michigan.

Henry had graduated from high school a year earlier, but unsure of either a major or possible career path and unprepared to leave his family, he decided to stay close to home and enroll at the University of

Kansas City. UKC, a small private school located near the city's famous Country Club Plaza, welcomed its first class only a few years before, in 1933. Despite the still-lingering effects of the Great Depression, the college grew rapidly. The expansion of the University of Kansas City was clear evidence of a maturing community. At nearly the same moment civic leaders built the university, the city also began a professional symphony company and an art museum. Many other hallmarks of urbane life—ballet, theater, research hospitals—were soon in place in the community. Adopting the more visible trademarks of cultural sophistication, Kansas City was beginning to shed the cowtown image so popular during Henry's childhood. Still, for all this development, the city and its university remained small. After a year at his hometown college, Henry now looked forward to the challenges and opportunities only available at a school like Michigan.

In contrast to the up-and-coming UKC, by the 1930s the University of Michigan was already an established powerhouse of scholarship, professional training, and innovation. The school was founded in 1817, more than two decades before the state was carved out of the old Northwest Territories. The first campus home was in Detroit, but by 1840, the university had relocated forty miles west to Ann Arbor. As a flagship campus for an expanding frontier region, the University of Michigan grew at a marked pace throughout the rest of the nineteenth century. In the first decades of the next century, the university added new buildings for a dental program and a pharmacy school, reorganized the engineering school, expanded the natural sciences and chemistry programs, and

Aerial photograph of University of Michigan, 1939.

constructed a performance center, new libraries, a hospital, and several dormitories. With an early emphasis on scientific research and with the support of a strong core faculty, Michigan became one of the most respected state universities in the nation, earning the nickname the *Harvard of the West*. In the 1920s, the school further expanded its national profile as it became a popular choice for bright Jewish students who, because of religious quotas limiting Jewish admission, were crowded out of many of the nation's top universities. In 1939, the year Henry arrived on the sprawling six-hundred-acre campus, the university maintained a robust enrollment of more than twenty thousand students.

Academic rigor and a reputation for religious tolerance no doubt influenced Henry's decision to transfer to Michigan, but family connections were, in many ways, equally important. Henry was named for his mother's beloved uncle, Henry Wollman. Like the Blochs, the Wollmans were midwesterners, and the two families remained close. In 1878, Wollman graduated from the University of Michigan Law School and, for the rest of his life, remained passionate about Michigan and its primary university. After law school, Wollman began his professional life in Kansas City as a circuit court judge before eventually settling in New York City where, in the early decades of the twentieth century, he built a successful legal and political career. A sought-after corporate lawyer, Wollman participated in a number of precedent-setting legal cases in the early twentieth century, including the United States Shipbuilding case, which burnished his reputation as one of the most experienced attorneys of his era. Wollman also became active in New York philanthropy (Central Park's famous ice skating center, Wollman Rink, is named in the family's honor). Without children of his own, Henry Wollman took a keen interest in the lives and educations of his many nieces and nephews. Indeed, when he died in 1936, his sister, Kate, followed through on a Wollman family promise to pay the college tuition for their grand nieces and nephews—as long as they chose Michigan. For Henry, it was an offer too attractive to let pass.

When Henry attended the University of Kansas City, he took a variety of courses, but at Michigan he

Henry Bloch, University of Michigan entrance photograph.

found his focus in the College of Literature, Science, and the Arts, especially the Mathematics Department. By his own admission, he struggled with languages and was forced into extra study for the required courses in the humanities, but he excelled in mathematics. He explained to family and friends that he enjoyed the challenge of solving equations and that thinking about complex problems often kept him, an obsessive underclassman, up late into the night. Henry made a wise choice with mathematics, as among the Michigan faculty were leading figures of the age, including Raymond Wilder, member of the National Academy of Sciences and future president of the Mathematic Association of America, and Herman Goldstine, one of the developers of the world's first digital computer. In an early letter home to his mother, Hortense (Horty) Bloch, Henry trumpeted, "On my math examination . . . I got a 97." He chided himself for losing three points on "a real careless mistake," but more troubling, he joked, was that his less-than-perfect score "broke my string of 100s, which went way back to last year." His achievement in the field continued throughout his career at Michigan, and, as he admitted late in life, "math was the only subject I was good at . . . . It was the only subject that mattered to me."

Henry soon recognized that his aptitude for math and numbers might very well influence his career path. In another letter home, he told his family of a 1941 field trip to Detroit. A big insurance company had invited his class to its company headquarters in hopes of meeting students interested in becoming actuaries. "It was just the opportunity I was looking for," he noted. "Actuaries are in great demand and ones with a good knowledge of mathematics receive very high salaries—up to $25,000 a year." A position with a large, urban firm did not materialize from this early visit, but it was clear that the ever-practical Henry, even at nineteen, was already searching for ways to connect his studies to a lasting career.

As the calendar changed from the 1930s to the 1940s, Henry was in an enviable position. He enjoyed his studies, his job prospects were bright, and he was increasingly drawn into an active social circle on campus. There were a handful of students in Ann Arbor from Kansas City and one of them, Jerome Grossman, was president of Zeta Beta Tau, a Jewish fraternity. Grossman encouraged Henry to pledge and, despite his father's advice to concentrate instead on his health and

Henry Bloch in fraternity. Fall 1942. Henry, second row, first on the left.

his studies, Henry joined the Zetas. The usual routine of collegiate parties, fraternity events, and, especially for Henry, bridge games, created a pleasant social atmosphere for Michigan undergraduates. Henry remained in close contact with his parents and brothers; his letters to them reveal a genuine fondness for his years in Ann Arbor.

In many ways, then, Henry's experiences at the University of Michigan appeared typical of the era. A glance at the university yearbook, *The Michiganensian*, reveals stories of football games against rival Ohio State and dances featuring bands like Les Brown and Tommy Dorsey. Essays about the latest homecoming queen, late-night study sessions at University Library, and cheeky student pranks reveal a thriving social environment. But significantly, the student publication also includes evidence that the campus political atmosphere was in transition. The first page of both the 1939 and 1940 volumes, for example, contained a picture of an undergraduate couple silhouetted against a colored sky and captioned: "To Peace." Yearbook editors cautiously noted that while "we realize that any immediate universal peace is more a dream than a reality . . . we believe that when all humanity dedicates itself to brotherly living, the world will experience the promise we have of 'PEACE ON EARTH GOOD WILL TOWARD MEN.'"

Such a dedication reflected the dominant attitude about war in America during the period. Many American citizens remembered the devastation of World War I, and, as they struggled to put the events of the Great Depression behind them, another global war was far from their minds. America in the interwar period deepened its commitment to neutrality, and politicians repeatedly resisted calls for increased military preparedness. Jazz, flappers, and Hollywood captured headlines, while citizens of the age put worries about global politics underneath the glitter of a consumer society. As events in Europe became more ominous, however, the climate on campus, certainly as reflected in the tone and timbre of the yearbook, changed. Soon the opening-page dedication to world peace was gone and in its place was an editorial about the grim political realities facing

Michigan students. "It is conventional to picture the graduate as facing shifting tides of fortune and to wish him courage and success in his voyage," the yearbook opened. "Today, however, these platitudinous phrases assume a portentous meaning . . . never before [has] the graduate faced a world in which the very way of life [sic] is threatened." The student editors of the yearbook defended the value of a liberal arts education during dark political times. A Michigan education, they reasoned, increased awareness of democratic values and "the traditions of a free people" that support human civilization, yet such applause came with a degree of caution as uncertainty clouded the future. Now, instead of a banner to peace, the yearbook was "dedicated to those who must and shall carry on."

This dutiful, somber patriotism permeated campus life, casting a pall over the typically carefree collegiate atmosphere. In a yearbook photo essay about Scabbard and Blade, the Army ROTC honor society, the group was described rather glumly by staff writers as a collection of young cadets dedicated to discipline, camaraderie, and the study of the "brutality and futility" of war. Such sentiment was even apparent in coverage of campus social events. Pictures of the Junior Hop Dance revealed respectful students gathered in a gym decorated with red, white, and blue streamers under a spangle-studded eagle. Coverage of a second dance, the year-end Senior Ball, was accompanied with the caption:

> Graduation time is always a peculiar mixture of sadness and pride, but this year more than ever, the outgoing seniors will be filled with misgivings about the next few years. Many . . . can look forward to a very difficult near future.

Even at a time of celebration, students were aware that troubling international events might influence their lives in profound ways unknown in America for a generation.

With growing concerns about German aggression in Europe, Henry—like most young men of that time—began to consider his options should war come to the United States. Many Michigan undergraduates were, the yearbook once again explained, "looking forward to a year's training in the service of Uncle Sam." A supporting photo essay revealed the seriousness of the situation. Young men, pictured at a local draft board, were described as participating in an exercise "more effective than a political course, fire-side chat or banner headlines [at] bringing World War II and national defense to the student's mind." Instead, draft registration was an event with "serious and personal" consequences.

Henry's interest in serving his country was firm. "I wanted to be part of the war," he later remembered. "I knew it was the right thing to do." But what form such commitment would take was still unclear. An avid reader of military studies, he knew the history of World War I, and the horrible stories about trench warfare made a deep—and unfavorable—impression. One result was that Henry had little interest in joining the infantry, even as he maintained his commitment to service. It was not until December 7, 1941, however, that the reality of his possible involvement in the war hit home. In the middle of a campus bridge tournament, Henry's game was interrupted when a student burst into the playing room shouting that Japan had just bombed Pearl Harbor. Cards scattered across the table as students ran to find a radio to hear the news reports out of Hawai'i first-hand. The next day, Henry gathered with other students to hear President Franklin Roosevelt declare that the United States was now at war.

After Pearl Harbor, Henry's thoughtful ponderings about possible service soon took on a new level of seriousness. In 1940, President Franklin Roosevelt had reinstituted the Selective Training and Service Act, making young men eligible for conscription in the army. But Henry had no desire to wait for the draft and instead began investigating the Army Air Corps. "I understood it would be dangerous," he later explained, "but I wanted to fly." The danger was no doubt part of the attraction, but no less significant was an Air Corps recruiting pitch that allowed soldiers to finish college before starting active duty. This promise was made popular in army advertising campaigns and recruiting propaganda, most notably the 1942 film *Winning Your Wings*. Directed by John Huston and starring Hollywood leading-man-turned-pilot James

Michigan students selling war bonds in Ann Arbor, August 1942.

Stewart, the picture profiled several young men, including college students, interested in the Air Corps with Stewart, dressed in his military flight suit, assuring each recruit that they could join the army and not disrupt their educational career. Drawn to the adventure of the sky and with a commitment to begin training after graduation, Henry enlisted in the Army Air Corps at the beginning of his final year at Michigan. After an early-semester conversation with one of his math professors, Henry thought he might even have a good chance of becoming a math instructor in the cadet training program after he had completed the required training courses.

The reality of war quickly changed this discussion and Henry's future. As casualties mounted in the early years of the conflict, the army could no longer wait for students to graduate. Statistics for the Eighth Air Force, Henry's eventual assignment, were grim. For more than three years—May of 1942 to July of 1945—the Mighty Eighth planned and executed the Allied bombing campaign against Nazi-controlled Europe. The result was an impressive record of accomplishments: more than four hundred thousand bomber runs and eleven thousand aerial victories. Among its servicemen, the Eighth counted more than 550 aces, 17 Medals of Honor, 220 Distinguished Service Crosses, and an amazing 442,000 Air Medals. The Eighth would pay a heavy price for this record. The Eighth suffered nearly half of the U.S. Army Air Force's casualties, including more than twenty-five thousand killed. The Ninety-Fifth Bomb Group, Henry's ultimate assignment, would face equally substantial losses. As wartime pressures escalated, officials from the Army Air Corps requested fifty thousand additional pilots, eleven thousand bombardiers, and nearly ten thousand navigators. The need for fliers was immediate and unrelenting. For young men like Henry, waiting for graduation was simply not possible. In the middle of the academic year, Henry Bloch was called up for training. His war had finally begun.

March 26, 1943

Dear _Mom_,

I'm sending this from the Army Air Force Classification Center here at San Antonio, Texas, where I arrived today. I was met upon arrival and am now here with the rest of the future Army Air Crews.

I've been registered and assigned to Cadet Squadron _109_ where I expect to remain until I am ready to enter a Preflight School. During this time I will have my physical examinations and tests which will determine whether I become a Bombardier, Navigator, or Pilot. After being classified and transferred to Preflight School, I will commence my actual preflight training, which will last for about nine weeks. As of today I am insured free of charge in the National Service Life Insurance, Veterans' Administration, Washington, D.C.

You will, no doubt, think it strange receiving this type of letter from me instead of a personal note, but here is why: Our Commanding Officer knows that during the excitement and process of getting settled during the next few days, some of us will be apt to forget to write to the folks at home. This is his way of letting you know where I am and that I am well.

I know I'll have more interesting things to tell you when I write a real letter. In the meantime please let me hear from you. My address is:

A/C _Henry W. Bloch_.
Cadet Squadron _109_,
Army Air Force Classification Center,
San Antonio Aviation Cadet Center,
San Antonio, Texas.

Please address your letters to me exactly as shown above, so that my mail will reach me promptly.

Henry's first letter home. Form letter from cadet training center in San Antonio, March 1943.

Training for War

In the early spring of 1943—as General George Patton led his tank corps into Tunisia, and German U-boats increased their attacks on Allied shipping in the Atlantic—Henry Bloch reported to the Aviation Cadet Center in San Antonio, Texas. In the early days of the war, all cadets arriving at classification centers like San Antonio had to meet stringent requirements for admission to the Army Air Corps. Candidates, for example, had to be young (twenty to twenty-seven), white, and unmarried. Further, each successful applicant had to provide letters of recommendation as evidence of "good character," have completed at least two years of college, and as a final hurdle, complete a series of demanding physical and psychological examinations. After Pearl Harbor, however, demand exceeded supply, and the army began a slow expansion of its ranks. New recruits to the Air Corps in the early 1940s now included many young high school graduates and older, married men. Letters of recommendation were no longer required, and, for the first time, African American applicants were accepted, although into a segregated program based in Tuskegee, Alabama. Despite the efforts of the army to enlarge the applicant pool, however, candidates entering classification centers were still subject to extensive physical and mental testing. High scores were required for all candidates hoping to become pilots, navigators, and bombardiers. The training process remained rigorous, and in 1943, the year of Henry's induction, nearly half of all applicants were unable to pass the required tests.

After arriving in San Antonio—in March of 1943—Henry's first letters home do not reflect the strain of army life, nor the stress of aviation training, but rather a remarkably positive response to the abrupt change from campus culture to active duty. Not long after getting settled

U.S. Army Air Corps aviation cadets during exams, circa 1942.

in Texas, for example, he wrote to his parents, "The best way I can describe this life is to say that it is great." He knew that these early weeks of training were "supposed to be the worst part of it all while we are here at the classification center, but I really love it. I'm with the best bunch of fellows you could find anywhere—they are just plain boys, some with practically no school and some with college degrees, some farmers and some from cities like Kansas City, Denver and Minneapolis." His fellow recruits, he concluded with a midwestern colloquialism, "are all swell."

In these letters home, he also gave his family a picture of daily life for new soldiers. The training center, he noted, included simple barracks, just two-story, wooden houses with forty recruits on each floor. The conditions were traditional army basic: bunk beds and shared footlockers with one transistor radio (that happened to be Henry's) that everyone enjoyed. Perhaps more surprising was his reaction to military food, a standard complaint of army life. The mess, Henry wrote, is "really great and all of it you can eat—ice cream every day for lunch."

Not even the intense schedule seemed to wear on him. His days began with 5:30 A.M. reveille and ended with a *lights out* call sixteen hours later. A near non-stop barrage of tests, drills, training exercises, and physical activity filled the time in between. The goal, Henry wrote home, is to get new soldiers "acclimated to the army routine." "Yesterday," he wrote, "we had 9 hours of stiff mental exams, and this morning I had my psycho-motor exam which was a lot of fun." Few recruits described the motor exams—tests that stressed muscular coordination, anxiety levels, and problem solving ability—as fun, but Henry enjoyed the challenge and, as he admitted, "so far I have done all right." He was concerned about an upcoming strength test, as he was told that it "is the toughest physical examination in the world," but he remained confident in his abilities.

As it turned out, Henry had little reason to worry, and he excelled in the San Antonio training program. One result of his strong performance was that he qualified for his choice of aviator position: pilot, navigator, or bombardier. In the Army Air Corps, pilots were most prestigious, and Cadet Bloch chose pilot training. Before he was able to tell his parents the news, they received a letter from Major General Brant, Commanding Officer of the training center, informing them that, "Your boy, now an Aviation Cadet, has been specially selected for training as a Pilot in the Army Air Forces . . . . Men who will make good material for training as Pilots are rare . . . . I congratulate you and him."

Everything was in place for Henry to begin his career as an army pilot. He would complete the requirements of the classification center, move to weapons training, then flight school, and finally get his assignment to an active military theater. Then his mother intervened. In a telephone conversation not long after his decision to train as a flier, Horty Bloch let her son know that she did not want him to become

HEADQUARTERS
ARMY AIR FORCES GULF COAST TRAINING CENTER
Office of the Commanding General

April 27, 1943   Randolph Field, Texas

Mr. and Mrs. Leon E. Bloch,
414 W. 58th St.,
Kansas City, Mo.

Dear Mr. and Mrs. Bloch:

In a memorandum which has come to my desk this morning, I note that your boy, now an Aviation Cadet, has been specially selected for training as a Pilot in the Army Air Forces.

In order to win this war, it is vital to have the best qualified young men at the controls of our military aircraft. Upon their precision, daring and coolness will depend in large measure the success of our entire war effort.

The duties of an Army Pilot call for a high degree of mental and physical alertness, sound judgment, and an inherent aptitude for flying. Men who will make good material for training as Pilots are rare. The Classification Board believes your boy is one of them and that he will in all probability win his wings as a military pilot.

You must realize, however, that all of our study of the problem has produced no infallible method of determining in advance whether a young man has that inherent something which will make him a natural and safe pilot. As a result, some pilot candidates are later transferred to other types of military training.

Comprehensive tests indicate that your son stands a very good chance of successfully completing the rigid training for an army pilot and you have every reason to be proud of him. I congratulate you and him.

Sincerely yours,

G. C. BRANT
Major General, U.S. Army
Commanding

Letter to Henry's parents from Commanding General Brant, April 27, 1943.

SAN ANTONIO AVIATION CADET CENTER
SAN ANTONIO, TEXAS

Dear dad,   Fri. morn.

What I am going to tell you is very important and will probably make you very happy. Since I have written some last I have been doing a lot of thinking and just now I have returned from the Faculty Board where I had my classification changed from a pilot to a navigator. This was a difficult change to make and I never thought that I could make myself do it, but as I said before I have done a lot of thinking and talked to many officers, and pilots who washed out. I'll try to tell you why I made the change if I have time before we mess drill.

First of all on my conscience is the fact that I swore to you and mother that I would do all in my power to be an instructor and obtain my degree. As to the first, as a pilot I am not sure just how and what I could teach and I wouldn't

Henry's letter to his father discussing the switch to navigator.

a pilot. It was not an unreasonable position. By 1943, all Americans were well aware of the heavy toll on Allied fliers caused by the German Luftwaffe and the Japanese Air Service. Horty wanted Henry to choose a less dangerous position. "If you become a pilot," she threatened, "your father is going to Washington, D.C., to get you out of the service." Of course, what she did not understand was that Henry did not have a safe option. Combat flying was, to state the obvious, dangerous for American pilots, but navigators and bombardiers—as well as everyone else in the airplane— were also in harm's way. Still, Henry, as a dutiful son, would do his best to put his mother's concerns to rest.

In a late spring letter to his father in 1943, Henry opened, "What I am going to tell you is very important and will probably make you very happy." He explained that after a great deal of thought, he had changed his classification from pilot to navigator. "This was a difficult change to make and I never thought that I could make myself do it, but as I said before I have done a lot of thinking and talked to many officers, and pilots who washed out," he wrote. He repeated to his parents the same conversation he once had with a Michigan math professor, explaining that his goal was to complete the training program and then become a stateside instructor. Given the desperate need for combat crews, such a goal was probably not realistic. The army had little interest in training flight crews only to let them remain stateside as instructors. But Henry held out this option, no doubt for the benefit of a nervous mother. "As I have said before," he reasoned, "I heard that the upper 10% of the class get to be instructors, so you can be sure that I am going to try as hard as I can." He admitted that a top score would be difficult, given the quality of his fellow candidates, but he tried one last time to put his mother at ease. "As a pilot my chances of getting killed while training would be pretty high," he admitted, "but as a navigator you don't need to worry, as I don't believe that anyone has died yet [during training]." By focusing on the rate of training accidents, Henry was technically correct, but in directing his parent's attention to training, he spoke little of the dangers that waited all cadets in combat. In closing, he explained that a final advantage of navigator training was that he would get his wings after "27 weeks [of training] instead of the 36 weeks [for pilots]," but this, too, was only a small consolation. "This letter is getting very long . . . and there goes the bugle," he ended, "so I'll drop this subject with the hope that this meets with your approval and also that of mother's."

Henry's compromise plan worked, and his parent's hesitation was, at least temporarily, put aside. In his next letter to his father, Henry thanked him for his understanding. "Yesterday I received your letter, and it made me feel good to know that you are glad that

I am in navigation. You are partly responsible for my change so I hope it meets with your approval." He continued to hold out the possibility of becoming an instructor, but his path was set as the once pilot trainee now became a navigator trainee. For Henry, the switch involved a great deal of thought and stress, but for the Army Air Corps, his decision was especially welcome, as by 1943, navigators were desperately needed in bombing units.

The shortage in trained personnel was, unfortunately for the Army Air Corps, ubiquitous. The army began preparation for war facing a number of real challenges. Gearing up a fighting force was a massive operation, and throughout much of the early years of the conflict, the Air Corps in particular was often in short supply of materials, equipment, and especially instructors. In 1943, more than fifteen thousand navigators completed the army training program, yet manpower was still a real need. New aircrews needed to learn flight-navigation techniques—dead reckoning, radio communication, celestial guidance, radar, and LORAN (Long Range Navigation)—from experienced professionals, but as the casualties of war mounted, finding seasoned instructors became more difficult. Acquiring appropriate training aircraft proved no less of a problem. The Air Corps employed a variety of aircraft for instruction, AT-7s, B-18s, B-34s, and C-10s, but it was a constant struggle to divert aviation resources from the battlefield to training. One result was that the Air Corps tried to maximize efficiencies as much as possible. Cadets were required to undergo one hundred hours of flying in both day and night conditions, completing a total of twenty-one flights. For each flight, they trained with three other cadets, a pilot, and an instructor in the plane, thus easing the number of aircraft that would otherwise be needed for one-on-one instruction. Still, the demand for planes and instructors was constant as Henry moved through the training program.

After San Antonio, Henry was stationed at the nearby Harlingen Army Gunnery School. The school, located near the border town of Brownsville, was carved out of Texas farmland in 1941. Fifteen ranch houses were torn down, and in their place came the well-known wood and tarpaper of hastily constructed army buildings. The mission of the school, first in a five-week program, later six, was to train army fliers in air-to-air and air-to-ground combat techniques. At the airfield, four nearly six-thousand-foot-long runways accommodated an impressive array of aircraft—AT-6s, A-29s, B-24s, P-63s, just to name a few—as new fliers and navigators received instruction in important combat skills. Cadets learned by firing at targets towed by other aircraft or by strafing fixed targets on the ground. All airmen, regardless of classification, learned how to shoot the .50 caliber machine gun, an anti-fighter, defensive weapon mounted on many army aircraft. Henry practiced on the Browning-made weapon so much he was able to take apart and reassemble the machine gun blindfolded. As in San Antonio, Henry found his training both exciting and rewarding. "Our life down here," he wrote to his mother, "is spent in turrets, handling guns, and shooting. We have skeet shooting every day, which I really like, and shoot out of turrets every other day." When he had the opportunity to shoot at targets in the air, he was elated. As he wrote to his aunt, "Today I had one of the greatest experiences I ever had, and it was wonderful." He explained that he was in an open-cockpit AT-6 and, as the pilot "did dives, rolls, and just about everything in the books," he was trying to shoot at a small target "tossed by another plane about 200 yards away." Shooting at targets—long nylon sleeves about twenty feet long towed by other aircraft—was a standard element of gunnery school. Each cadet manned a machine gun loaded with colored pellets. At the end of the exercise, their scores were calculated on how many of their colored "bullets" hit the airborne target. Henry had yet to get his daily score, but as he admitted to his aunt, "I am sure that my gunnery was terrible." Once again, Henry humbly undersold his abilities, as he passed his gunnery exam with the highest possible score, earning an experts medal in the process. His performance at gunnery school led to an instructor offer, a nice prize in the middle of a war. He turned it down. The instructorship came with a lower rank, and, from the moment of his induction, Henry had his mind set on a higher goal.

His training regime, then, would continue with preflight instruction for navigators. His days were even longer than his first stressful weeks in San Antonio. He wrote a detailed letter to his parents describing the daily routine. His day, he explained, "begins at 5:10, awfully early, with lights out at 10 P.M." Just five minutes after reveille, he was expected to be in formation, dressed in uniform, and ready for drills. They drilled the recruits so much, he noted, "you know the commands before they are given—but everything must be precise." Time not spent on drills was devoted to physical training. It was, he remembered, "really tough—much more than I anticipated." On his first day, the men "had 30 minutes of solid calisthenics followed by running over the obstacle course . . . followed by a mile run." He had ten minutes to shower and dress for classes to follow. The nine-week course was intense, and recruits were given one small perk: no KP (kitchen patrol) duty, but the physical fitness and class work were demanding. His note to his parents explained the class schedule as if it were items on a grocery list: "48 hours of code, 20 class hours of mathematics, 17 hours of naval forces (facts about the navy), 10 hours of ground forces (facts about the army], 24 hours of physics, 18 hours of maps which is navigation, 18 hours of aircraft identification, 9 hours of chemical warfare, and 8 hours of first aid."

"We are kept busy," he noted dryly, "but the work is interesting."

In other letters home, Henry told his parents that in spite of the demanding schedule, he continued to enjoy military life. "I can't begin to describe how interesting everything is," he explained. His class time was spent covering "everything a soldier needs to know." Such instruction included preparation for the dark realities of war—he wrote his mother about "lectures on how to hate the enemy" and how to "take pride in killing a Jap or Gerry"—but most of his letters reinforced his affection for the military experience. He did well at each of his training stations, and he met a wide spectrum of men, most of whom fell outside his usual circle of Kansas City or Ann Arbor acquaintances. He told his father about "a boy who has done nothing but bum around the country in freight trains . . . getting jobs where he could and always looking for excitement. He's a real fellow, and we go around together quite a bit." He described another "wonderful fellow" who was "a graduate of Minnesota with his Ph.D. from Chicago who was a Professor in Political Science . . . before the war." Fortunately he was also able to find some "very fine bridge players"—he continued to enjoy bridge during the rigors of training. Once again, Henry admitted that he even liked the food, especially after a detachment from the Women's Army Corps took over the mess hall. A few weekend border hops to Mexico provided much-needed relaxation and, as he concluded to his mother about army life, "I must confess that with the exception of getting up at 5, I honestly think it's the greatest place in the world." He admitted that "things are very strict and they ask a lot of you, giving in return [next] to nothing . . . [but] the army can be the way you make it."

Such an attitude served Henry well, and he was committed to maximizing every opportunity. "I made up my mind that when I got here I was going to be right 'on the ball' and I have been," he noted. "Doing everything the best I could and working 'till I was exhausted and cursing the officers" paid off with a "spotless" record and a "conscience free." His model work ethic led to "many responsibilities in the training of others, making the future look bright." It took sacrifice, he admitted; he had given up much to study and to become a better soldier, but in the end, "the army appeals to me."

Henry was so dedicated to military life that in one of his last letters home before leaving for additional training, he adopted the language of an army spokesman, encouraging his family to support the war effort with the purchase of war bonds. "Did you see where the 3rd War Loan Drive has started? You know, you folks can do as much as we can by investing in War Bonds." He noted that the "weakest generals and the poorest fighting men" will not lose if they have enough supplies. There was little reason to worry about the quality of the troops. "They have proved themselves," he said, but victory required support from the home front. "The more you and the rest of the people like you invest, the sooner I and millions of other sons like me will be home." Henry ended his plea with an apology—"I hope this doesn't sound too much like a sermon"—but he knew "every word of it is true." Still an energetic cadet, Henry was, of course, correct. The men and women in uniform depended on American industrial supremacy for the weapons, aircraft, and munitions required to wage a global war. The Allied victory in World War II was a product of both the literal might of the U.S. Armed Forces and the manufacturing prowess of the American home front.

A few weeks after he sent off this message, in May 1943, Henry was ready for his final training program. Navigation flight school would take him back to where he began his training, outside San Antonio and Hondo Field. As he admitted to his parents, he was nervous about his next assignment. A strong performance was expected if he was to receive his lieutenant's commission, he explained. "Keep your fingers crossed." In this eighteen-week program, cadets received instruction in a wide variety of navigation methods, including dead reckoning. Dead reckoning enabled flight personnel to determine aircraft position from the record of course flown, distance, and drift. The method seems straightforward, but flight navigators had to

Hondo Airfield students learning navigation training, circa 1943.

use a variety of sources of information—maps, radio, meteorology, sextant readings, celestial navigation, and radar—to establish navigational position. In all of this, navigators also had to be adept at determining weather conditions and able to read maps quickly and accurately. Any error when determining position could spell disaster on dangerous missions. To minimize such mistakes, navigational training included exposure to in-flight instrument reading, position reporting, code reading, and, in cases of emergency, how to bail out of a damaged aircraft.

These lessons were learned in more than one hundred hours of flight time. Training began with four-hour flights eventually building to eight-hour training sessions, and finally, several flights designed to simulate combat situations. After his first flight, a six hundred mile trip across Texas in early October 1943, Henry wrote to his aunt about the experience. With two other cadets and an instructor in the airplane, Henry acted as navigator and felt the pressure to perform mistake-free. The pilot "will fly anywhere

Navigation cadets learning celestial navigation techniques, Hondo Airfield.

the navigator tells him to (that is, within certain limits) and it is awfully easy to make some little mistake in your computation and find yourself flying in a course opposite to the one you intended to go." After just his second training flight, Henry wrote home to his father about two cadets who had been sent to the hospital and three who had already left the program because of low ground-school averages. In a second letter to his mother, Henry confided, "The work is tough and the barracks [are] emptying fast because of the washouts." Several weeks later, Henry gave another update with similar results, explaining to his father, "Washouts here have practically emptied the barracks, over a 3rd of our class has washed out (because of academics and air sickness)." Despite the increasing intensity of his training, Henry continued to do well. At the midpoint of his flight school, Henry was given more complicated navigational problems, describing one such flight over the Gulf of Mexico to his father:

> We took off, climbed to flight altitude, and flew until we received word that an enemy vessel had been sighted at a certain point going in a certain direction. We began an interception problem, but the boat was not sighted so we patrolled the ship's course. Still no boat so we turned on a search pattern to cover the area the boat was believed [to be] in. After spotting the boat we turned on another course and flew on it as long as possible and yet made another turn to return to Hondo with the gas tank empty (that is, down to the reserve line.)

In his flight training and classroom exercises, Henry, as he had done at his other stations, enjoyed the experience. More than a third of the cadets who started the program did not complete their training, often receiving an infantry reassignment. Cadets were frequently examined, and trainees were expected to maintain a seventy percent average to stay in the program. Henry's average, he reported to his family, was "in the nineties" although he "won't be satisfied until it gets higher."

Flying twice a week, studying for ground exercises and classwork, keeping up with his military duties, and, of course, trying to get a little sleep, kept Henry "so busy that during the week I have absolutely no time off." Earlier in the training protocol, candidates were given free Sunday afternoons. "But now," he explained, even this short break "is rare." In a follow-up conversation with his father, Henry repeated that "I've never been so busy in my life." It was time well invested, however, and after performing at a very high level at navigator school, Henry graduated from flight training. He had one last station before his entry into war: MacDill Air Base in Tampa, Florida.

MacDill, originally known as Southeast Air Base, Tampa, was first established in 1939. Soon after the war erupted in Europe, American military officials grew concerned about the threat of German submarines on American shipping in the Gulf of Mexico. The United States was not yet in the action, of course, but thousands of tons of American supplies, especially oil from refineries in Louisiana and south Texas, were bound for England from the Gulf ports. To protect American naval and commercial vessels throughout the Gulf, then, air defense flying operations began at MacDill in 1941. With the entrance of the United States into the conflict, the primary object of MacDill shifted to the training of bombardment units

MacDill postcard, 1941.

bound for the European theater. A number of different aircraft patrolled the skies above MacDill, including the B-26 and the B-18, but the workhorse of the Air Corps was the B-17. It was here in central Florida that Henry became familiar with this aircraft that would be his wartime companion and saving grace.

When Henry Bloch entered the Army Air Corps, he was part of a new strategy for waging war. In no previous conflict did military strategists rely so heavily on the use of aerial bombing as they would in the Second World War. World War I introduced the world to aerial weaponry, but despite the hyped legends of aviators like Germany's Manfred von Richthofen, Canada's Billy Bishop, and the American David Endicott Putnam, aircraft during the Great War were too small, too limited in range, and too imprecise to impact enemy targets from the air. New technological innovations in the interwar period, however, made air combat a central factor in Allied plans for victory, and few of these advances were as significant as the development of heavy bombers like the B-17.

The B-17 was an unusual aircraft in that it was both large and fast. In the 1930s, engineers at Seattle's Boeing Airplane Company began work on what would become the B-17, nicknamed the *Flying Fortress*. The Air Corps needed an aircraft capable of reinforcing distant bases, such as those in Hawai'i and Alaska, while carrying heavy payloads at speeds of at least two hundred miles per hour. Boeing, and a number of other aviation companies, tried to build the appropriate aircraft, and in a 1935 competition, Boeing's B-17 prototype—equipped with four large Pratt & Whitney radial engines—captured the attention of army officials. Even after a deadly crash involving Boeing's first prototype, the Air Corps began placing orders for the aircraft, and production accelerated in 1936. Less than two hundred B-17s were in army service at the time of Pearl Harbor, but a recent order for more than five hundred bombers stood as evidence of the increasing significance of this aircraft. As a testament to its importance and versatility, the B-17 would eventually achieve

B-17F assembly line, 1942.

the highest production rate for large aircraft in the armed services and see action in every combat theater during World War II.

The B-17 had several distinctive features. Known for its swooping dorsal fin, the bomber first appeared in European combat operations in August 1942. With its hundred-foot wingspan, the B-17 appeared immense, but its interior space was surprisingly cramped for the ten-person crew. Fliers often compared the close quarters to that of a submarine. A thin aluminum skin covered the structural ribs, also manufactured of aluminum, with thousands of rivets providing strength and durability. The aircraft was solid enough to endure long distance campaigns, but at the same time, the skin itself was thin enough that a well-placed screwdriver could poke holes right through it. As one WWII veteran remembered, it was like flying inside "a lightweight aluminum cigar tube."

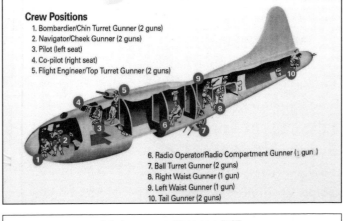

Crew Positions
1. Bombardier/Chin Turret Gunner (2 guns)
2. Navigator/Cheek Gunner (2 guns)
3. Pilot (left seat)
4. Co-pilot (right seat)
5. Flight Engineer/Top Turret Gunner (2 guns)
6. Radio Operator/Radio Compartment Gunner (1 gun)
7. Ball Turret Gunner (2 guns)
8. Right Waist Gunner (1 gun)
9. Left Waist Gunner (1 gun)
10. Tail Gunner (2 guns)

Interior crew positions on a B-17.

Each crewman had domain over a distinct section of the aircraft's cramped metal geography. The pilot and copilot sat in the bomber's top position, surrounded by instruments in what was, in essence, a five-foot cube. The instrument panel allowed them to monitor fuel pressure, altitude, wind drift, airspeed, position, and direction. Importantly, the pilot team could perform all the calculations required for keeping on course toward the bomb site. Underneath the cockpit in the nose compartment on the port side, the navigator sat at his desk with charts and instruments underneath a pair of windows and an astrodome, a transparent dome fitted into the aircraft to allow the use of a sextant during navigation. Ahead of the navigator was the bombardier, who sat in the most exposed position, behind the bombsight and beside the switch that controlled the doors to the bomb bay. Right behind the cockpit was the top turret with twin .50 caliber guns manned by the technical sergeant, who served as the plane's engineer and chief mechanic. The rest of the crew included two waist gunners, a tail gunner, a gunner in the plexiglass belly turret, a radio operator who sat in a sealed cabin that also contained a .50 caliber machine gun, and, later, a radar navigator who operated a guidance system. In 1943, the version of the B-17 that Henry used would be equipped with thirteen guns and powered by four turbo-charged engines capable of producing more than twelve hundred horsepower. Their combined power propelled the craft at speeds up to 250 miles an hour, where the B-17 climbed to twenty-five thousand feet—while carrying an eight-thousand-pound payload on a thousand mile journey.

The belly of the beast was the bomb bay, where bombs were stacked from floor to ceiling. It was the responsibility of the bombardier and top turret gunner to remove the safety pins that prevented the bombs from accidental detonation when loading. For all of the advanced technology in the aircraft, if any problems came up, the crew was responsible for fixing the issue manually. If the bomb bay doors would not open or shut, a common problem due to hydraulic failure, crew members had to crank the doors by hand—a terrifying and dangerous experience for the gunner.

Still, for all of its problems, the B-17 developed a reputation for resilience against enemy fire. The aircraft was sturdy enough that it could withstand buffeting winds and tough weather and, more important, often lumber back to home base with only one working engine. Each Flying Fortress returned to battle, mission after mission, even after punishing blows that would have doomed a less-durable machine. As to be expected, for many crew members then, the rugged B-17 earned a place in their hearts that transformed it into much more than a plane. It was a valued partner in a war that took a terrible toll on man and machine. To call the B-17 *significant* is an understatement. Military historian Donald L. Miller described the B-17 as "an elegantly engineered aircraft, suggesting both power and movement. Menacing looking on the ground, it was beautiful to watch in the air."

One of the key innovations that made the B-17 so effective was an advanced sighting system, the Norden bombsight. Developed by Carl Norden, a Dutch engineer who arrived in the United States in the early years of the twentieth century, the bombsight helped flight crews more accurately acquire ground targets. Military planners knew as far back as the early years of WWI that getting aircraft perfectly level before releasing the payload presented a fundamental challenge for aerial bombing raids. A slight variation of only one or two degrees could produce dramatic errors in targeting. Norden's bombsight incorporated elements of the gyroscope, first designed for ships at sea, to help with leveling and accuracy. Improvements to the sight better calculated drift, drop angles,

Norden bombsight.

and altitude to make precision strikes a possibility for American flyers. Even in the midst of war, many citizens objected to bombing campaigns that killed large numbers of civilians. With improved technology and strike capability, in part made possible by the Norden bombsight, American enthusiasm for aerial combat increased over the course of the Second World

War. Norden's invention was first used in the spring of 1943 and, while problems of accuracy were not completely gone, the bombsight soon became a standard element of the American war machine.

The B-17 and its advanced technology certainly gave the American armed forces an advantage, and the nation's commander in chief, Franklin D. Roosevelt, understood the significance of aerial power. The president, a navy man at heart, believed—even as many Americans clamored for peace in the late 1930s— the nation would inevitably enter the conflict. Once committed to war, Roosevelt believed that air power could well decide the outcome. Convinced that only massive numbers of planes could defeat Hitler's growing menace in Europe, FDR developed a military industrial machine capable of producing a staggering number of war planes. In January of 1942, just after the Japanese attack on Pearl Harbor, the president poured new resources into the American aerial war effort to help the Allies push back the Axis attack. With strategic bases located in eastern England, the Army Air Corps would carry out bombing operations throughout the European theater. It was a chaotic and dangerous world and one that Henry would soon become intimately familiar with.

Off to War

After a brief ten-day leave back to Kansas City, Henry arrived in Hoboken, New Jersey, a newly minted second lieutenant, ready to head overseas. His training had taken more than a year, and now he gathered with several thousand fellow soldiers—each equal parts nerves and excitement—eager to begin their war. At the appointed hour, he boarded the RMS *Queen Elizabeth*, one of the largest ships in the world, bound for Europe. The *QE* made the ocean crossing as quickly as possible. German submarines continued to patrol the Atlantic, and a nervous tension descended on the large vessel as she zigzagged through open water, hoping to avoid U-boat patrols. Six days after departure, after traveling across the ocean at speed, the *Queen Elizabeth* moved slowly up a foggy loch lined with the distinctive emerald-green hillsides of Scotland. The destination was the dock station of Gourock, a small port town thirty miles west of Glasgow. Troops disembarked and were quickly dispatched by train and troop trucks to dozens of service posts throughout Great Britain and beyond. Henry, too, did not linger long in Scotland, as he was soon on his way to Horham, a small Suffolk village in East Anglia.

Had Henry arrived in Horham just eighteen months earlier, he would have found a small English village seemingly unchanged from the previous century. Indeed, the town probably appeared exactly how many American soldiers—familiar with romantic images from picture post-cards—thought the English countryside was supposed to look. The Church of St. Mary, with its famous bells and small graveyard covered in wildflowers, anchored one end of the village square. A Christian church had sat on that ground since the early thirteenth century. Tidy thatched-roof houses, some nearly seven hundred years old, were sprinkled throughout the rest of the main green. A number of other buildings from the fifteenth century, young by Horham standards, were arranged across the village commons. A steady popu-

B-17s on the Horham runway with grazing sheep.

66

lation of a few hundred people patronized a handful of small shops and a pair of pubs found along the main avenue. An iconic English, red telephone booth stood as one of the only reminders that modernity had come to this part of the empire. Even after the war had begun, daily life appeared relatively undisturbed. But the world was coming, even to Horham. By the time Henry arrived, German V-2 rockets had recently struck not far from the village, German POWs, trucked in to work local farms, were now a common sight, and in place of fruit cellars, local residents had constructed bomb shelters to protect against German air raids.

With the construction of the bombing base, Horham would change once again. The village was selected as the permanent home for the Ninety-Fifth Bomb Group, one of three air groups that formed the Thirteenth Combat Wing of the Eighth Air Force. The Eighth Air Force was created at the Savannah Army Air Base in Georgia, less than a month after the Japanese bombed Pearl Harbor. From the very beginning, the group trained for an attack on Germany. Its goal was to use air strength to prepare the way for a land invasion that would mark the American entrance into the war. The Eighth would use its primary aircraft, the B-17 Flying Fortress and the B-24 Liberator, to win the air battle and, hopefully, turn the tide of the war. Henry and the rest of the Eighth Air Force would provide much-needed reinforcements to the British

Royal Air Force (RAF) that had been bombing German targets since 1940.

The logistical challenges required to build an aerial attack force were—in classic understatement—large. The army needed more than seventy airfields capable of accommodating sixty combat groups and as many as three thousand aircraft. With the strength of the German war machine showing little signs of weakness, everything had to be built urgently. What happened at Horham was representative of how American military planners incorporated large expanses of the English countryside into the Allied war effort. To create this important air base, for example, army engineers cleared more than eight square miles of English countryside. Hundreds of trees and hedgerows that had stood for generations were removed for new roads, water mains, and sewers. Heavy trucks ran around the clock delivering the nearly two hundred thousand yards of concrete required to construct new runways. Unlike many of the temporary wood and tar-paper structures Henry had seen in his Texas training, the army was now building substantial brick structures; Horham, constructed to withstand bombardment, was here to stay. Soon the base looked like a small American town, complete with all the amenities required for army life. Mess halls, movie theaters, chapels, a post exchange, as well as bars and an officers' club were in place. The addition of a finance office, a medical unit, a weather detachment, an engineering group, as well as detachments of firefighters and military police completed the transformation of the base. For the original citizens of Horham, peaceful country living was replaced with the beehive activity of military life.

Aerial photograph of Horham Airfield.

Henry and the rest of his comrades were not the first to occupy the base. The Royal Canadian Air Force was assigned to Horham in 1942, but soon, the Ninety-Fifth Bomb Group arrived and established their presence in the skies over Europe. From the first, members of the Ninety-Fifth would see almost continual action, including D-Day, stretching right up until the closing moments of the European conflict. Such extensive engagement across so many theaters also gave the Ninety-Fifth an unfortunate honor. The Ninety-Fifth would lose the highest number of aircraft of any Allied bombing group. The group would also see more than six hundred soldiers killed in action, nearly two hundred wounded, and more than eight hundred captured as enemy prisoners of war. One result of this cruel wartime math was that Henry's group was the only bombardment group to receive three Distinguished Unit Citations (a special award given to combat units for extraordinary heroism in action). The first, earned for an attack on an aircraft assembly plant in Regensburg, Germany, under intense enemy assault, came on August 17, 1943. The second came from a frantic, but ultimately successful, bombing raid on the Münster marshaling yards in the fall of that same year, and the third came from action in March of 1944. On that early spring day, the Ninety-Fifth was one of many groups assigned to a daring daytime raid on Berlin. The RAF bombed German targets almost exclusively during nighttime hours but the Americans executed the more dangerous daytime raids. These brazen daylight attacks marked a dramatic escalation in the Allied aerial war strategy. On this particular sortie, heavy weather and severe enemy resistance on the journey to Berlin forced the other groups to turn back, but the Ninety-Fifth continued on and scored a strategic and symbolic victory against the German capital. The group would also deliver food to starving Dutch citizens, fly supplies to the French Resistance, bomb oil fields in eastern Europe, and fly support missions to Russia. In total, the Ninety-Fifth flew many hundreds of missions and strategic bombing sorties and played a critical role in the air campaign in the European theater.

Henry's introduction to life with this noted group was, however, anything but bright. On the day of his arrival in Horham, he was directed to his assigned Nissen hut, a semi-cylindrical steel structure used throughout the war to house army personnel. Shown to his bunk by a base guide, Henry noted that it was still covered with the personal belongings of another flier. With a quick sweep of his arm, the guide nonchalantly cleared off the bed, explaining to Henry that the bunk's last owner was shot down earlier in the day. Welcome to the war, son.

Before his duffel was unpacked, then, Henry began his first mission. This was not a bombing raid but rather the challenge of building a flight crew. Many American flight crews trained together as a group in the States before going abroad, but Henry was assigned to his Horham crew without any prior experience. The ten-man crew was forced to bond quickly and completely, as the pressures of war fell hard on the newly constructed group. Often for combat flight crews who operated in a near constant state of high stress, the bond between the men made the pencil-

Photo of flight crew. Back row, left to right: Milton Carlton, Joseph Pisarski, Joseph Eldracher, Joseph Straub, and William Fenley. Front row: Henry Bloch, William Greene, Frank Psota, and Warren Kalbacker.

thin difference between success and failure. The plane's commander, the pilot, was Frank Psota, from Cicero, Illinois, a suburb of Chicago. Before the war, Frank was a student at the University of Chicago, working as a campus policeman to help pay for tuition. Although he could not know it at the time, his part-time, civilian job would intersect in a significant way with his military future. On one of his regular night patrols of campus, he was ordered to guard the spectator stands at Stagg Field, the university's football stadium. As this was such an unusual assignment, Frank asked what was going on. His supervisor told him that it was nothing important, but he was to make sure that no students entered the area. Frank's surprise increased when the watch commander then gave him a .45 pistol. When he arrived at the stadium, he noticed that campus maintenance workers had constructed a special room inside one of the squash courts under the bleachers. Sandbags and bricks lined the walls of the space transforming the court into a fortified, albeit makeshift, laboratory. As Frank quickly surmised, this was no ordinary patrol assignment. He was, for example, required to sign in everyone who entered the room, now being used for scientific experiments. Frank's log soon included names like J. Robert Oppenheimer and Enrico Fermi, the leading international scientists of the day. Frank connected the dots and realized that he was patrolling the laboratory where these scientists worked to split the atom, an essential step in the construction of an atomic bomb. One day in the school newspaper, Frank read about their successful experiments with nuclear fission. The very next day, he and the rest of the part-time, student policemen were replaced by two busloads of officers, each armed with machine guns.

Campus police work paid Frank's bills, but his real passion was aviation. Always interested in flying, Frank had mastered gliders and began pilot training with the Army Air Force. Even though he passed the instrument test, he was dismissed because an eye test revealed that he was colorblind. However, as the demand for pilots increased during the war, the Army

Air Force revised the vision requirements so that his "color confusion" was no longer a disqualification, and Frank was back in as a pilot.

The copilot was Warren Kalbacker from Greenport, New York, a historic seaport community located on the north fork of Long Island. At age twenty-two, Henry was the youngest member of the crew. Kalbacker, at twenty-eight, was the oldest. He had graduated from high school a decade earlier and had, for a time, driven a truck. Like his pilot Frank, however, Warren wanted to become an air force flier, but, lacking college training, he was unable to apply. After the war began, the air force began to open the requirements for flight school, and Warren, largely studying on his own, was able to pass the entrance examinations. Tall and dapper with a striking mustache and a penchant for wearing white, silk flying scarves, he was too large to qualify for a fighter plane but was successfully recruited to join the bomber ranks. Once with the team in Horham, Kalbacker's piloting skills became a key reason for their success.

The balance of the crew consisted of bombardier William H. Greene, described by all who knew him as genial and easy going; the radio operator, James L. Fenley; Milton R. Carlton, top turret gunner; Edward D. Pisarski, ball turret gunner; Joseph F. Eldracher and Warren K. Peterson, waist gunners; and Joseph. J. Straub, tail gunner. Together, these young men would face the challenges of war while also getting to know each other, their aircraft, and their assignments.

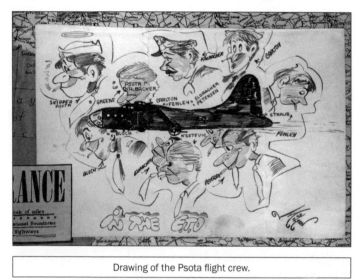

Drawing of the Psota flight crew.

In the spring of 1944, when Henry arrived at Horham, military commanders were focused on the land invasion in Europe. The exact date of the main thrust had not been determined, but all military strategies, including coordinating the aerial attack, were aimed at weakening enemy forces to help Allied soldiers push through to Berlin. With that objective achieved, American officials hoped the end would finally come to the war in Europe. In the early days of American involvement in the war, the Eighth had a different mission, however. Their goal was destroying Germany's offensive capabilities, targeting submarine-repair facilities, ball-bearing factories, and aircraft-production plants. While this initial bombing campaign was not as successful in limiting German production as Allied war planners had hoped (aircraft facilities were, for example, often hidden in forests or underground), the big bombers were more effective in a much more dangerous goal—that of luring out German fighters, where they suffered heavy losses from American and British attack forces. By one estimate, Germany lost nearly one-third of its single-engine aircraft and, more significantly, almost twenty percent of its experienced pilot corps. Still, even with these losses, German defenses in 1944 remained formidable, and finding a way to breach the protective shield the Luftwaffe had placed over Europe fell to the Mighty Eighth.

The bombing campaign in the European theater, however, was never without controversy. Although no doubt hard for today's readers to understand, certain rules of engagement dictated action in the world wars. Prior to the outbreak of World War II, the so-called *laws of war*—supported by various Geneva Conventions—governed such items as the treatment of prisoners of war, the prohibition of certain destructive weapons, and outlawed the targeting of civilians. The development of new instruments of aerial warfare complicated these guidelines, and most nations at war did not view the restriction of aerial bombing as a wise military strategy. Still, at the outset of the conflict, President Franklin Roosevelt asked all belligerent nations to limit their air raids to military targets. The British and the French agreed; so, too, did the Germans, although the Nazis reserved the right to strike at what they deemed to be fortified cities. In the early summer of 1940, the significance of this exemption was made clear.

In May, Luftwaffe bombers hit Rotterdam in an effort to force the Dutch out of the war. The target was not the Dutch forces stationed outside the city but the urban center. The bombing raid leveled more than twenty-five thousand buildings—homes, schools, warehouses, hospitals—and left nearly one hundred thousand residents homeless. In the aftermath of this attack, England's Royal Air Force stepped up its bombing of civilian and industrial targets. English fliers increasingly targeted German oil refineries, factories, and rail yards. Such escalation, in turn, led to more frequent German attacks on Allied cities. In the early months of this back and forth, and in an effort to encourage England to accept peace, Hitler prohibited attacks on large cities and civilian populations. When peace was not forthcoming, however, German bombers struck the outskirts of London. Once again, in an expected response, the RAF then moved against Berlin in late August 1940. The immediate result of this ever-fluid choreography of battle was the German blitz on London in September. Over the course of the next eight months, the Luftwaffe would hit the English capital more than seventy times. Other cities like Birmingham, Liverpool, Bristol, and Glasgow would also be targeted from the air. For what it gave, Germany would be repaid in kind with massive assaults by Allied bombers. The air portion of World War II, once hoped by many observers to play only a small role in the conflict, was now a determining factor in which side would win in the end.

It was into this messy conflict that American fliers like Henry Bloch and the rest of the Eighth Air Force entered. The escalating aerial battles of the early war years shaped American involvement in the conflict in ways few of these young men understood. Many of these soldiers no doubt missed the immediate connection, but the runways for Horham were constructed from the wreckage of London. Throughout the blitz, English officials were continually clearing London's streets of debris. It was then transported by rail to East Anglia where it was ground into concrete and poured into tarmacs. Every time Henry's bomber lifted off from one of these repurposed runways, it was his job to shift the balance of power. Thanks to the American air assault, it was now the Germans who were forced to sift through the rubble of their once untouchable cities.

Missions

In the spring of 1944, the Ninety-Fifth Bombing Group was focused on Berlin—Germany's capital, the sixth largest city in the world, and the most formidable target in Europe. Striking Berlin was no easy task. The city sat more than five hundred miles from the closest American airbase and had a defensive shield of Luftwaffe fighters and heavy ground defenses, especially anti-aircraft rockets. Hitler, Hermann Göring, and other top Nazi military planners had repeatedly announced to the German people that Berlin would never suffer attacks from Allied forces. After such bravado, a hit on the city by the Allies would send a powerful message about the future of the war effort. To their credit and against steep odds, England's RAF had bombed in and around Berlin beginning in 1940. These first raids were conducted during the day and, given Berlin's stout defenses, resulted in unacceptably high losses of British aircraft. Early in the campaign, then, the RAF made the tactical decision to switch to night sorties, but, as much as aircrews welcomed the cover of darkness, they also found it impossibly difficult to strike the city with any precision at night. One result was that during much of 1940 and 1941, the impact of these raids on Berlin was limited. Soon, the RAF shifted the focus of its aerial assault to German U-boat ports and facilities. Berlin remained a prized target, but U-boats ravaged trans-Atlantic shipping, denying the Allies access to much-needed supplies and materials. Berlin would have to wait.

In late 1943 and early 1944, English forces would once again turn their attention to the Third Reich's capital. With the launch of the Battle of Berlin, the city was renewed as a priority target. The RAF planned a number of attacks on the city that resulted in hits to residential areas, rail systems, and war-production facilities located near the city's center. In these raids, a wide swath of devastation left perhaps as many as 5,000 residents dead with 550,000 others homeless. Despite this tally, however, civilian morale in the city did not break, nor were essential urban services disrupted. Even German war production, the main thrust of the RAF assault, was not constrained, as industrial output continued to rise throughout the rest of 1944. Most significantly, this latest series of attacks once again cost the English Bomber Command heavily. Throughout the five-month battle, the RAF lost more than five hundred aircraft and 3,500 men.

Without significant debate, military historians now regard the Battle of Berlin as a failure for the Allies. If Berlin were to fall, it would be up to the Americans.

In February and March of 1944, with the RAF exhausted, the Eighth Air Force would take up the challenge. In the early evening of March 4, fourteen American bomber wings (wings consisted of several groups of planes) took off bound for Berlin. Like the early attacks sponsored by the English, this first American raid struggled with heavy weather and stiff German defenses, but American aircraft did reach the city, inaugurating a new level of engagement in the western theater. It was this attack on Berlin that led to the first unit citation for the Ninety-Fifth. The citation was reason for great applause, but few airmen in the unit probably recognized at that moment that this was only the beginning of a tough fight. Just two days later, for instance, on March 6, another American attack on Berlin came with a high cost. Nearly seventy B-17s were lost. In the spring and summer of 1944, the escalation of the German air campaign continued to extract a heavy burden on American flying units. Even as the number of sorties increased, and the targets became more diverse, Berlin remained one of the most dangerous combat assignments for the Ninety-Fifth.

Henry was in the final stages of his stateside training program when American military planners turned their attention to Berlin, but he would be part of this attack all too soon. On the afternoon of April 28, 1944, not long after his arrival at Horham, Henry gathered with several other fliers as the base commander hoisted a red-alert flag in the squadron area. All present knew its meaning: mission tomorrow. The posted mission plan listed crews by pilot, and, scanning down the list to *Psota*, Henry knew he was on for his first combat flight. Even for experienced crews nearing the end of service, the night before every mission was filled with anxious anticipation. In their own way, soldiers did their best to relax, perhaps with beer in the officers' club or a movie. Henry often marked the time with a card game or a quick letter home. Sleep, however, was always difficult. As Charles Lajeskie, a pilot in the Ninety-Fifth who, like Henry, was preparing for his first mission, later explained, "I suppose I was just too nervous and apprehensive because all I did was toss and turn restlessly on my bunk, worrying and pondering the possibilities and probabilities."

While Henry and his mates fought through a fitful night, much of the base was active in preparation for the mission. Logistical planning for each assault was extensive. In the base intelligence room, where large maps of the active fronts hung on the walls, the planning team charted the exact flight course in red thread. This team not only plotted course and direction but also reported on weather, expected resistance levels, and logistical support. As intelligence officers prepared for the morning briefing report, many other soldiers performed the dozens of tasks both large and small required to get the American bomber groups airborne. Crews in fuel trucks rumbled from one aircraft to another, filling the B-17s' massive tanks. Armorers examined and tested weapons, especially the .50-caliber guns, and loaded the many needed crates of ammunition into each aircraft. Bomb loaders brought ordnance from storage warehouses located on the far side of the base and carefully prepared each aircraft's bomb compartments. In a base outbuilding, a team of technicians prepared the B-17s' aerial cameras that were so critical for intelligence and reconnaissance work. A second group of technicians prepped the all-important Norden bombsight, loading the instrument into the aircraft nosecone. The most conspicuous activity on the base came from the mechanics who, like so many insects, crawled over the bombers checking power, propellers, and engines. The quiet of the English night was continually interrupted as every engine was started for a required preflight warm up. Airmen got used to much of the noise but never the early-morning firing of the large engines. Remembered one veteran of the Ninety-Fifth, the chorus of revving engines was less a "lullaby" and "more a portent of bad things to come."

At 3:00 A.M., an enlisted man went to each hut to rouse the crews. A fast shower and shave followed with a breakfast of eggs, coffee, and toast was complete by 4:00 A.M. The flight crews then divided. Pilots, navigators, and bombardiers attended their specific

instructional briefings. Crews were informed about flak areas, fighter escorts, expected ground defenses, and, of course, the target. As the pilot Lajeskie recalled, "quite a roar went up . . . when the curtain concealing the large-scale map of Europe was drawn back

Horham navigators in early morning briefing meeting.

and . . . we saw the colored yarn extended all the way to Berlin." Henry's first mission would be an attack at the heart of Hitler's Germany. In the navigator conference, Henry was given mission check points, but the briefing officer did not need to remind him of the danger involved. This every member of the Ninety-Fifth already knew.

At the conclusion of the morning briefings, each crewmember was directed to the supply depot to receive flight gear. On top of their standard-issue, olive-drab boxer shorts and T-shirts, the airmen donned wool khaki shirts and pants, a pair of heavy socks, and silk gloves. In addition, soldiers on a B-17 received fur-lined boots and an electrically heated flight suit and matching gloves. As enclosed and pressurized bomber cabins became more available, flight crews found the added bulk increasingly unnecessary, but preparing for the unexpected—which often occurred at thirty thousand feet—meant that many flight crews opted for the extra protection. Finally, crewmen grabbed their parachutes, harnesses, oxygen masks, and Mae West life jackets. In case their plane went down, each crewman also holstered a .45-caliber sidearm. Fighting your way out of Germany with only a pistol was hardly ideal, but it was better than the alternative.

Fully equipped, the men made their way to the flight line and their assigned aircraft. On this April morning, Henry and his team arrived at a Flying Fortress nicknamed *G.I. Issue.* Had Henry known that this would be the only time he would fly in this aircraft, his gentle nervousness would have no doubt been replaced with a feeling more serious. Once at the aircraft, each team member performed the final required flight checks. Joe Straub, tail gunner, received the mission's formation diagram from the pilot and then checked the plane's oxygen systems. Straub was also responsible for the signal lamps and flare pistols, one of the only available ways to communicate with other planes once in the attack formation. He also checked in with the radio operator, James Fenley, making sure the communication system was in working order. As radio operator, Fenley was responsible for determining the estimated target-arrival and base-return times for each mission. He was also to check on the plane's various communication systems, making sure that the plane's radio, or *interphone*, worked for every crewmember. Fenley also maintained the aircraft's defensive countermeasures, including *chaff*. The British called it *window*; to the Germans it was *duppel*; but whatever the label, chaff was designed to fool ground radar. Chaff consisted of small bundles of aluminum strips, each about twelve inches long. At several appointed points in the mission, Fenley would release small clouds of chaff that, once in the airstream, would separate into small pieces, every one showing up on German radar as a possible aircraft. As a result, anti-aircraft guns found it difficult to separate these decoys from real B-17s. Henry never understood how "little pieces of aluminum foil" could distract German guns, but he was thankful for the technology that no doubt saved American lives.

The top turret gunner, Milton Carlton, doubled as the lead mechanic. He, too, examined the important oxygen system, as well as the aircraft fuses, bomb bay, and the machine-gun turrets. Keeping the many systems of the bomber operational while defending the aircraft from his top position would keep Carlton occupied throughout the whole of the mission. The waist gunners, Joseph Eldracher and Warren Peterson, climbed on board and immediately set to work double-checking the bomber's emergency equipment—oxygen backups, spare fuses, first-aid kits—making sure that the aircraft was ready for any unforeseen complication. Edward Pisarski, ball-turret gunner, examined his immediate world, the guns, making sure that the .50-caliber weapons were properly mounted and ready. His was a most precarious job, as the ball turret hung only about eighteen inches above the runway in the belly of the aircraft. In tight and very exposed quarters, protected only by a glass bubble jutting out from underneath the aircraft, Pisarski folded himself into the turret and would continually scan the horizon for enemy aircraft.

While the rest of the crew checked and re-checked systems operations, the pilot, Frank Psota, and copilot, Warren Kalbacker, conferenced together in the cockpit, going over an extensive preflight checklist. They inspected all flight controls, fuel gauges, throttle levers, as well as the proper movement of flaps, wings, and props. Kalbacker marched through his individual responsibilities and examined the bomber's brakes, generators, and secondary flight gauges. The bombardier, William Greene, examined the plane's payload, studied images of the target from multiple angles, and prepared the Norden bombsight for use.

Henry's task as navigator was to know every single turn and point on the mission, both out and back.

Such a task is simple to describe but complicated in practice. As he had learned in his months of training in the Texas desert, bomber navigation was an exacting art that demanded a quick mind as well as an in-depth knowledge of mathematical calculations. Every moment that required a change in course, altitude, or air speed fell to Henry to call. He was also to be aware of changing weather patterns and how to find alternative airfields if needed. But once again, Henry's chief responsibility was to know exactly where the aircraft was at any given moment along the designated bombing route, even when the unexpected conditions of war forced the aircraft to take evasive action. In this work, approximations were not good enough. For the mission to be successful, the B-17 needed to be accurate down to a quarter of a mile. For much of the flight, Henry sat in the nose section of the aircraft at a small desk, what he once described as "just a small piece of rough wood," behind and to the left of the bombardier. On his desk, covered with maps and charts, were the tools he needed to safely plot the course out and then back home for the rest of the men. Above his working table were mounted two important instruments: the magnetic compass and, just to its right, the radio compass. The radio compass was connected to a loop antenna located forward of the bomb bay and to a fixed antenna, slung along the bottom of the nose. The signal received by these two antennas would show up on the compass face as a relative bearing. From there, Henry was able to perform additional calculations to determine the accuracy of their aircraft's position. On the opposite side of his table was the drift meter. This optical device was used to determine the angle between the heading of the aircraft and its course over the ground. Henry needed to continually calculate drift, especially the impact of high altitude winds, to keep the bomber on point. When his aircraft came under direct attack, Henry was also expected to man the two .50-caliber machine guns stationed on either side of his compartment.

B-17s ready for takeoff.

With preflight responsibilities complete, crew members would wait. And wait. Many airmen considered this the most trying part of any mission. Some fliers performed pre-take off rituals, many others prayed. Henry's pilot, Frank Psota, recalled, "We prayed, we crossed, we did everything [we could]." Henry, the only Jew in a flight crew of practicing Catholics, was happy to participate in any ritual if it meant more protection in combat. Other preflight behavior had a more personal flavor. Henry remembered that Frank, who had gotten married shortly before leaving for England, had a lipstick case given to him by his new bride. Before takeoff of each mission, he made a small mark on the back of his hand for luck. Sometimes the wait for takeoff was only a few minutes, at other times it could stretch over an hour. On some days, as the crews waited, weather or other factors led to a scrubbing of the mission, leaving the airmen exhausted from the stress. But when takeoff

The control tower at Horham.

time was finally approved, Horham's flight control quickly moved into high gear. The control tower contacted the aircraft with taxi and positioning instructions, and each group arranged for the mission to come.

To get the full combat wing airborne required timing and precision. At Horham, bombers were scheduled for takeoff at thirty-second intervals. After a very short roll, pilots advanced the throttles to full open, as the copilot called out air speed and distance. It was here, in the opening minutes of a mission, that pilots faced their first real challenge. Horham's runways were only about five thousand feet in length, leaving flight crews a limited window to get sixty thousand pounds of men and machine airborne. More than seventy years later, Henry still remembers the taxi on this, his first combat flight. "We had a very heavy load," he explained. A few seconds after going full throttle, their plane began to "zig zag down the runway." At the end of Horham's primary strip was a large ditch, so not getting up meant serious trouble. As the pilot and copilot struggled to regain control of the aircraft, Henry remembered thinking, "I thought we'd had it," but finally, "at the last minute, we got her up." The crew was able to power the bomber into formation, but it was an important lesson for these rookie fliers.

As the planes gradually rose up, they turned and formed into increasingly larger groups: first into groups of three aircraft, then into squadrons, and finally into a configuration of multiple squads. Each level of aircraft continued to spiral upward until the skies over Horham were filled with bombers. Such flight patterns were necessary to reduce the chance for mid-air mishaps, but it also allowed the aircraft time to form into proper command wings. Gradually the various pieces of the aircraft puzzle came together until a wing of more than one hundred aircraft finally banked east and turned toward Europe.

Heavy bombers from the Ninety-Fifth heading toward Germany.

The combat groups of the Ninety-Fifth flew in a formation known as *LeMay's combat box*. Named after Colonel Curtis LeMay, then commander of the 305th Bombardment Group, the combat box was a tactical formation used by heavy bombers throughout the war. Also known as the *staggered formation*, the box allowed bombers to maximize defensive capabilities by massing the B-17s' weapons while at the same time increasing the offensive output of these squadrons with a coordinated bomb release on concentrated targets. The plan stacked bombers at different altitudes in a diamond-shaped formation that was easy to fly and control, while also reducing exposure to flak. Such tight formation was not without problems. Prop wash, or wake turbulence, caused by so many aircraft in such a limited flight space ensured that many bombers had a rough flight to their target, but the added protection that came from the box was worth the risk associated with heavy turbulence. Once in formation, fighter escorts accompanied American combat wings to their targets. Early in the war, the limited range of fighters reduced their ability to provide protection to American bombers. Later, however, improvements in fuel technology meant that aircraft like the P-47, the P-38, and by early 1944, the P-51 ensured that no Axis target in occupied Europe was safe from American bombers. Bomber formations often took hours to assemble, and as a result, the faster fighter escorts left their bases at a later time and met up with the combat wings shortly before crossing into enemy territory. With their high cruising speeds and increased maneuverability, the fighters hovered on the flanks above the bomber formations, ready to swoop down and engage enemy aircraft.

Escorts did their best to cover their bomb wings until the full group reached the Initial Point, or IP. When the combat group reached the IP, most often an easily identifiable landmark about twenty miles or ten minutes of flying time before the target, the escorts peeled back and the bombers made their final approach to the drop zone. From that point on, the bombing groups flew straight, level, and took no evasive action. "We were ordered to go to the target at any cost," Henry explained. As one pilot from the Ninety-Fifth recalled, "This was the sweating time." Mission plans called for all planes to drop their payloads simultaneously in tight "wingtip to wingtip" formation. The B-17 did not release bombs as singles but rather in groups known as *sticks*. Once each bombardier acquired the pre-selected aimpoint, he began the release sequence, and five-hundred-pound bombs would rain down on the target. Such methods made the bombers lethal, yet it was also during the final leg of the bombing raid that the aircraft was the most vulnerable to the enemy. After dropping their bombs, the planes, now several tons lighter, lurched upward, banked sharply, then turned back toward the fighter escort and, hopefully, England.

On this April mission, Henry and his crew were part of twelve combat wings built from three bomb divisions of the Eighth Air Force. They were protected by sixteen groups of American fighters, including P-51s, P-47s, P-38s, and two squadrons of RAF Mustangs, all set to attack the center of Berlin. Intense flak separated one bomber division from the LeMay formation and made completing the raid difficult for the entire wing. One pilot in Henry's combat wing surveyed the scene and remembered, "Everything was quite serene until we crossed the enemy coast, where we saw our first bursts of flak—ugly, brown-black blobs off in the distance . . . . As we approached the Initial Point," he continued, "we could clearly see the huge cloud of flak over Berlin that we had to fly through in order to reach and hit the primary target." Henry's recollections from that day were nearly identical. "Intensive flak was everywhere," he reported. "The skies filled with flak .... We were hit multiple times." Each strike, he said, "was swift and sharp, tearing through the plane's skin." What seemed like "thousands of pieces of metal just went right through our plane," he noted. The smell was intense enough that even through his oxy-

B-17 encountering Axis flak, December 16, 1943.

gen mask he could detect the odor of hot metal. Not yet to the target, Henry began to wonder, "How many blows could our plane take?" Fortunately for the crew of *G.I. Issue,* the aircraft was not yet near its breaking point. Looking back at the experience, Henry concluded simply, "The B-17 was well made, really well made." Despite strong German resistance, the main thrust of the attack force dropped nearly fifteen hundred tons of bombs on Berlin-area targets, including strategic rail lines, the Tempelhof airport, a marshaling yard, and the German Ministry of Aviation.

From the pilot's seat on the *Fire Ball Red,* Charles Lajeskie described the bombing run into Berlin as "quite frightening, as bursting flak shells appeared to be all around our plane." After the bombs were away, his aircraft took "a barrage of hits, and almost immediately the number three engine ran away and had to be feathered." *Feathering* meant turning the propellers edge front to reduce drag. Down an engine, his aircraft could not keep up with the returning group formation and was forced to make it back to base "quite alone." After what he described as a long return flight, Lajeskie's crew "made it home safely, late, weary, and rather nervous."

In a situation eerily similar to what Lajeskie experienced, Henry and the rest of the crew on the *G.I. Issue* also found themselves unable to keep up with the formation. At the IP, bombardier Greene opened the bomb bay doors in preparation for release, but after their run was complete, the doors would not close. Now with the added drag, the aircraft began to lag behind the formation. Psota upped the speed to full throttle, placing great strain on the engines, but soon they were flying alone. In such a situation, the navigator became a vital member of the flight crew. When flying in a large formation, the navigator on the lead plane set the heading for the combat wing. The individual navigators continued to maintain positioning information, but their primary task was to keep their aircraft in proper alignment in the combat box. In this standard scenario, Henry would regularly inform the pilot of their position and the estimated time to various checkpoints, including the IP. But when out of formation and with no lead plane to follow, it was up to Henry to get the aircraft back to Horham. The consequences of even the simplest error were grave. As Henry explained, when bombers "fell out of formation . . . they were easy prey for the Germans." When, years later, he was asked if he was frightened, Henry replied that he was too naïve to be scared. "It was my first mission . . . I didn't know from nothing." He did know that they were "losing altitude, running out of fuel," and England seemed a long way off.

With three ruined engines and a fourth sputtering on fumes, Henry did get the crew back to base, shattered by the fatigue of combat, but safe. Years later Henry added that this was the only time— on his first mission no less—that he felt he deserved a medal. It was an incredibly dramatic day and a momentous

Bomb impact on German targets.

introduction to the war. "I never felt more useful," he explained, and when they touched down at Horham, he "was completely wiped out." After they completed their mission de-briefing, the crew celebrated a successful raid on Berlin. Although Henry usually found relaxation in a bridge game, that evening he joined the rest of the crew with a well-deserved drink. The crew had ample reason to toast good fortune, but the bombing raid exacted a hard toll on the combat wing. Attacking high-value targets like Berlin meant that the Americans paid a heavy price. Records from the Eighth Air Force reveal that this was one of the more costly runs of the entire war. The Germans, too, suffered severe damage, as one of Berlin's primary rail stations was hit and, more important, perhaps as many as ninety Luftwaffe fighters were lost. While the Americans mourned their losses, they would be back the following day as strong as ever. With available supplies of aircraft and skilled pilots declining, the Germans, by contrast, were slipping under.

Flight crew debriefing after mission, Horham.

The raid on Berlin changed Henry. Never knowing what the next day would bring, he decided to simply focus on the job at hand. "I would give it my all," he concluded. He would have ample opportunity to practice his new philosophical position. The crew was up again two days later, this time headed to

Sarreguemines, France, an important, river-port city near the German border. Next, it was the French community of Laon, a village that could trace its history back to the rule of Julius Caesar. Throughout this long history, Laon had faced invasions from the Franks, Vandals, Huns, Normans, Henry IV, Napoleon, and now the Nazis. Four more raids in quick succession in early May took Henry twice to Belgium, to the oil fields of Czechoslovakia, and then to Osnabrück in northern Germany, the home of Erich Maria Remarque, author of *All Quiet on the Western Front*. These raids targeted oil refineries, steel mills, railroad yards, and a Volkswagen plant. Military war planners used Allied air power not only to wear down the German military directly but also to limit their ability to produce the fuel and supplies needed for the Nazi war machine.

Just four weeks after his first raid on Berlin, Henry had completed ten missions. To the handful of original members of the Ninety-Fifth who were still stationed at Horham, Henry was a *newbie*, but he hardly felt like one. The experiences of the past few weeks were remarkable. Bridge games in Ann Arbor seemed incredibly distant and his home in Kansas City even more so. Two months earlier, he had been flying *milk runs* over the Gulf of Mexico, now he was part of a massive, industrial war machine. By early summer 1944, Henry thought he had seen everything the war could offer, but the biggest days still lay ahead.

Ath Air Force Buttle

Authority NND 745005
By RLS Date 06/22/0

Was this ship loaded with Nickles_____ Camera **YES**

Type_____ Photos Taken **Yes**

How many packages dropped_____

Combat Mission Interrogation
463rd Bombardment Group (H)

Always Give:
95th   Time-Place-Altitude

DATE · *Aug 8th*
TARGET · *Buzau*
BOMB LOAD · *16x250*

SQUADRON **412** SHIP NUMBER **237882**

POSITION IN FORMATION, **#3** *1083-*
2 CP 15 Lo WG-

PILOT · *Peota*
CO-PILOT · *Kaubacher*
NAVIGATOR · *Bloch*
BOMBARDIER · *Greene*
RADIO · *Fexley*
TOP TURRET · *Carlton*
R/W GUNNER · *Eldbacher*
L/W GUNNER · *Bond*
BALL TURRET · *Peterson*
TAIL GUNNER · *Straub*

IF MISSION NOT ACCOMPLISHED GIVE
REASON? IF TURED BACK GIVE REASON
AND COORDINATES:

16 x 250

BOMBS DROPPED ON: *Primary* TIME: *1115* ALTITUDE: *20600* HEADING: *300*

BOMBS JETTISONED (WHERE?)   BOMBS BROUGHT BACK (WHY?) *none*

WEATHER OVER TARGET:

BOMBING RESULTS: *A/D Very good results.*
good Concentration - N with hangars + workshops =
4509 - 2648

	Intensity	accuracy	Type
FLAK AT TARGET	Intense	Accurate	Heavy ✓
	Moderate ✓	Fairly ✓	Light
	Scant	Accurate	

OTHER FLAK AREAS: (Use one word
Location Coordinates   Intensity   Accuracy   Type from above)
none

_____

FRIENDLY A/C IN DISTRESS OR A/C DOWN:
none

OBSERVATIONS:
1. Target: A/D = 8 hangars - swi E of Buzau
4507 - 2651 = large fresh counate E-W Runy

A sample mission report from 1944. Flight crews filed reports on weather, enemy activity, and effectiveness of attack after each bombing mission.

Day of Days

In the near darkness of early morning, June 6, 1944, as Henry took his usual seat in the Horham briefing room, the intelligence officer told the men, "Today is the day." Rumors of a cross-channel invasion had been swirling around England for weeks, and it appeared that finally the time had come. In popular memory, D-Day—*Operation Overlord*—conjures up images of thousands of Allied ships crossing the channel under heavy steam, and equally famous pictures of numerous American GIs wading ashore against Nazi guns. Before the first landing, however, the Eighth Air Force was already at work reducing German defenses on assault beaches, paving the way for the Allied attack. Indeed, important attacks in preparation for the invasion occurred weeks earlier. In the second week of May, for example, Henry flew bombing raids against fuel plants in eastern Germany. The destruction of these depots deprived the Germans of much-needed supplies and pushed Nazi reserves to the limit just as the Allies mounted this critical offensive. On D-Day, virtually every functioning plane in the Mighty Eighth was in the air. The morning started off sunny and bright under cloudless skies, but toward noon the perfect flying conditions ended as the weather turned poor— even for an unusually wet English summer. A low ceiling of gray rain clouds marked the horizon, but as one Horham radio crewman remembered, on this day "Our B-17s [flew] even when they shouldn't."

According to declassified briefing reports, Allied military planners hoped that heavy bombers from the Ninety-Fifth would "knock out enemy strong points" including "coastal batteries, military headquarters and choke points on military roads." Hitting these targets in force, it was believed, would also "force enemy gunners to keep their heads down . . . before and during the actual landings." In the navigator briefing meeting, Henry learned that hitting the Germans dug in at Normandy would not be easy. The briefing report noted that the "targets are small" and "close together in many places." They must be "pinpointed exactly if they are to be hit," the intelligence report continued. "There will be no second runs on those targets; they must be identified on the first pass." The report ended with a special emphasis: "Ground troops are counting on us to knock out these targets. We must not fail them." Flight crews knew that American lives on the beach depended on precision strikes from above.

B-17s line up for takeoff.

Despite the early hour, Horham was soon a cluster of activity. While heavy bombers prepared to "soften" the French coastline, a naval invasion force of some 7,000 vessels—1,200 warships, 4,000 landing craft, and 2,000 support ships—readied to cross the channel. Beginning around midnight, Allied mine sweepers plowed into the channel, clearing the path for the landings to follow. Not long after, approximately 1:30 A.M., paratroopers from the 82nd and 101st Airborne divisions dropped behind German lines with instructions to secure key bridges, road crossings, and important French villages. American fighter planes were also at the ready as military officials looked to create an "aerial umbrella" above the landing zones capable of keeping German aircraft at bay. At 3:25 A.M., the lead group of bombers from the Ninety-Fifth took off from Horham. Just under two hours later, when the combat wing was fully assembled, the massive formation veered away from England and toward the French coast. With usual military precision, combat records from Horham's operations division note, "Landfall was made on the enemy coast . . . at 0654 ½" and "bombs were away" moments later. A second bomb group, flying at fifteen thousand feet, was right on the heels of the first, and according to the base operations officer, their "bombs were away upon landfall at French coast . . . at 0701." From the ground, the assault must have seemed endless; just as the mayhem of one bombing run concluded, another wave of Flying Fortresses appeared ominously over the channel.

During one of the day's early runs, Henry looked out the nose cone over the bombardier's shoulder and saw the full expanse of the Allied armada heading for Normandy. At a D-Day commemorative event decades later, he still remembered how moved he was by the sight of so many "boats" all drawn together. Other flight crews recalled a similar scene. A pilot from the Ninety-Fifth recalled how, "You could have walked across the channel on ship decks." A second flier reported "nothing but ships from one horizon to the next." A third air crewman reported that seeing "the whole invasion fleet, in daylight, on its way to the beaches of Normandy" was a "sight . . . an extraordinary feeling that all of us will never forget."

This first wave of bomber raids, designed to support Allied landing operations, focused on Nazi strongholds between the French cities of Le Havre and Cherbourg. The early morning runs were conducted through a "heavy undercast" (an opaque layer of cloud cover) that required the bombers to conduct their raids on navigational instruments. The reduced visibility made bombing Normandy all the more dangerous. Allied ships steaming toward shore and paratroopers massing just behind German lines made any loose targeting disastrous. The second mission followed a similar course, pushing over the beachhead, attacking targets further inland. Both groups returned to Horham by 10:30 A.M. where ground crews prepped the aircraft for another run. As the B-17s were readied, a combat wing of B-24s was dispatched against the city of Caen. Known for its rich history dating back to the reign of William the Conqueror, Caen was an important crossroads junction less than ten miles from the coast. The heavy fighting on D-Day, including this bombing run, enacted a large toll on the city. But control of Caen's strategic crossroads was critical to Allied objectives. A few

Navigator at work in B-17.

hours later, B-17 bombers from Horham, part of the fourth mission of the day, were once again dispatched against a number of tactical targets near the landing zones.

Throughout the day, the Ninety-Fifth bombed enemy coastal defense installations, knocked out railroads and switch stations, smashed bridges and inland roads, and targeted ammunition warehouses and radar towers. As pilot Frank Psota recalled, "We bombed . . . anything we saw moving," hitting trucks, tank cars, armored vehicles, barges, and

B-17 dropping bomb load on Nürnberg, Germany, 1944.

naval vessels. Unfavorable weather limited the effectiveness of the high-altitude bombing runs, but the impact of the Allied campaign on German troop locations as well as on supply depots and enemy morale was still significant. The Germans spent much of 1942 and 1943 constructing the famous Atlantic Wall, a series of coastal defense fortifications extending from Norway to the Spanish border. Hitler conscripted almost a million French citizens to build the defense system—mortars, artillery stations, ditches, land mines, pillboxes, gun placements—claiming in Nazi propaganda broadcasts that the wall was unbeatable. Within hours of the Allied invasion, however, the formidable *Atlantikwall* was in tatters. By nightfall, 150,000 troops were already ashore. Casualty numbers were also high, nearly ten thousand, but a beachhead more than fifty miles wide was now in American hands. Within a week, half a million soldiers entered the French breech and were fighting their way to Berlin. In the final assessment, the Mighty Eighth achieved their goal, "to gain air supremacy over Western Continental Europe in preparation for and in support of a combined land, sea, and air movement across the Channel and into continental Europe." A new chapter in World War II had begun.

The pace of D-Day was extraordinary, but in reality, the Allies had just a foothold in occupied France, and the bombing raids needed to continue. Henry and the rest of the flight crew were up again the very next day with another run to Normandy. The pace continued for the rest of June as they conducted additional aerial assaults to Misburg, a major railway hub in eastern Germany, to Nazi supply depots near Bordeaux, France, and to a steel plant near Hannover. Looking back at the flurry of activity, pilot Frank Psota was amazed at how much the crew flew. During one heavy stretch, he remembered, the crew "flew seven (missions) in a row" where, after landing, "They give you a big shot of whiskey," a quick meal, a few hours of sleep, and then "wake you up and you go on the next one." This unrelenting pace dampened the crew's outlook, if not their resolve. Psota later recalled somberly, "None of us expected to be alive." But personal expectations were always subordinate to collective duty, which consisted of simply doing your part, day after day, mission after mission, until the job was done.

As the month came to a close, crew members got a slight reprieve as they drew a different kind of assignment. Rather than deliver bombs to the enemy, they brought supplies to the Resistance. The story of the French underground is immortalized in the classic of American cinema *Casablanca*, but the reality is not far from the Hollywood legend.

After a blitz assault in 1940 by the Germans, French forces surrendered in June. It appeared to much of western Europe that the Nazi war machine was unstoppable. In exchange for a promise from the Germans not to dismantle French society, the French Prime Minister Henri Philippe Pétain, a World War I hero, surrendered and set up a collaborationist puppet government in the central French city of Vichy. At first, life in occupied France seemed little changed, but increasingly brutal German policies fostered growing resentment and hostility from French citizens. Germans forced French citizens to pay the expenses of the occupying German army; the Nazis transferred French laborers to German war factories in growing numbers; the collaborationist Vichy regime began rounding up French Jews for deportation to concentration camps. Another direct result of the German takeover was a floundering economy and growing social distress. When combined with the news that the Nazis had tortured and executed French citizens, the resentment against the German presence reached new heights.

Inspired by the exiled French general Charles de Gaulle, a patriotic resistance movement originating from the ranks of everyday citizens rose in response. Men and women from all walks of French life began to participate in small acts of sabotage—cutting telephone wires, defacing posters, slashing tires—against German forces. As the movement grew in size, it also expanded in scope. French mail carriers "lost" packages destined for German officers, telephone operators intercepted or garbled military orders, and Resistance spies infiltrated the Vichy government. Others contributed to the cause by publishing underground newspapers that supported a covert intelligence system or by creating escape networks for Allied soldiers and downed flight crews trapped behind enemy lines. Splinter groups organized in many French districts, often escaping into the countryside or the mountains out of reach of their Gestapo hunters. These cells became increasingly bold, destroying bridges, railroad stations, and executing armed assaults on German soldiers. Made up of a motley collection of socialists and communists, priests and students, and patriots drawn into France from across Europe, the French Resistance became experts at a unique form of modern guerilla warfare.

For all their successes against the Germans, the Resistance was continually short of resources. Allied forces, especially American bomber groups, began to aid the Resistance by bringing in equipment and supplies. Soon after D-Day, for example, American B-17s dropped radios to Resistance fighters so that Allied war planners could learn of German troop movements and locations. As the summer of 1944 wore on, these supply drops became more frequent and more vital to the success of the underground. Henry was part of one such mission when, in late June, he flew from Horham with a small wing of thirteen bombers to deliver food, weapons, and war materials to French Resistance fighters. On a clear day, the group crossed the English Channel and took a heading toward southern France. As the group approached the drop point, flying at low altitude, the bombers sighted three bonfires—the predetermined signal—and dozens of gathered rebels. As the crew of Henry's aircraft lowered the plane's rear door, strung parachutes, and prepared to drop tons of supplies, they paid little attention to the small-arms fire and flak coming from nearby German soldiers.

Wasting little time after the drop, the full group banked north and headed back to England. For Henry and his comrades, it was, finally, a calm day in the middle of an intense war zone. The respite was short lived, however. As soon as they returned to Horham, they entered right back into the fighting. The next target was a familiar one for members of the Ninety-Fifth: Schweinfurt, Germany.

On two earlier occasions, the Eighth Air Force had hit Schweinfurt, the site of a large plant that produced many of the ball bearings vital to the German war machine, and because of its value, the city was heavily fortified. The first bombing raid, August 1943, conducted under adverse conditions, led to the loss of more than two hundred airmen and the first unit citation for the Ninety-Fifth. The second attack came two months later, October 14, with equally devastating results for the Air Corps. The city's anti-aircraft batteries punished the American bombers with bruising results. By one scholar's estimate, the Eighth Air Force lost twenty percent of its aircraft on raids against Schweinfurt. During these aerial assaults, the heavy bombers faced stout, German defenses often without fighter cover. The area was beyond the range of American fighters, and the Luftwaffe simply waited for the fighter escorts to return to their bases, leaving their bomber wings unprotected. Based on the experiences striking at locations like Schweinfurt, the

Army Air Corps rushed into development plans to increase the range of American fighter planes. One result was the addition of a seventy-five gallon drop fuel tank that fit under each fighter wing, which increased range and opened new areas of Germany to heavy bombing.

When flight crews in Horham were told that Schweinfurt was once again a target, anxiety fell over the briefing rooms. The history of bomber raids on this city was well known among the Ninety-Fifth. As crews made it to the flight line on July 19, 1944, the mood was unusually somber. Henry remembered, "Schweinfurt carried the reputation—rightly deserved—of the most dangerous city in Germany to attack." To fly over the city, he concluded, "felt like getting a death sentence."

Despite the addition of fighter cover, the July 19th bombing of Schweinfurt proved as harrowing as before. Henry remembered that the aerial combat above the city was the most intense of the war, like a scene drawn from *Hell's Angels*, a 1930 Hollywood movie about aerial combat in World War I. To a reporter from Chicago, Frank Psota described the attack on the Bavarian city as the crew's most unforgettable mission. It was, he began, as if "the entire German air force met us" in the skies over the city. "I saw the biggest dogfights of my life," he concluded. "We lost close to 60 airplanes total, including Fortresses and fighters . . . . We got the

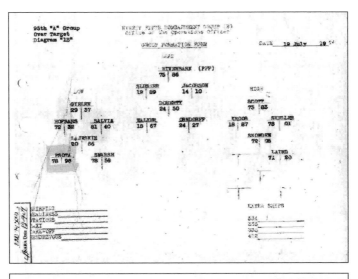

Mission records illustrate the position of each B-17 in the attack formation (LeMay combat box). The Psota plane is at the bottom left.

heck shot out of us." In the mission report Psota prepared after the crew returned to Horham, he indicated they had encountered flak over the city that damaged the aircraft, but their plane was relatively lucky. The post-flight report also noted how flak and anti-aircraft guns brought down a B-17 directly in front of them. He counted nine parachutes, but the ultimate fate of that crew was unknown. Nearly all the other postflight reports from the bombing group echoed his own. Aircrews described bursts of flak everywhere with wounded aircraft falling from the sky. The *milk run* to the Resistance fighters was already a distant memory, as Henry and the rest of the crew were right back in the thick of it. Schweinfurt lived up to its reputation as a dangerous target, but, unlike the previous attacks, this mission had a different ending. Aircrews from Horham reported heavy smoke rising from the target. Psota explained that the aerial combat over Schweinfurt was brutal, but concluded succinctly, "We destroyed the place."

B-17s in flight.

By the conclusion of the assault on Schweinfurt, Henry had transitioned from being one of the Horham rookies, part of the replacements brought in to shore up a bomber group desperately short on flight crews, to one of the base veterans. Schweinfurt was mission number twenty-four, getting close to the number of completed missions required to finish his tour. Successful missions to Lützendorf, Germany, and then three more to France in quick succession in late July and early August put Henry's mission count even higher. Although superstitious fliers would never say these words out loud, Henry and the rest of the crew began to think that they might get out of Europe alive after all.

Before that could happen, however, Henry and the crew had one last challenge. In the first week of August, the flight crew got word that it was selected for an unusually long bombing raid. Throughout 1943 and 1944, Germany responded to Allied air assaults by moving key industries, especially oil refineries, out of range of American bombers. Germany had extensive coal reserves, but oil, the most prized commodity of the war, was in short supply. As the war dragged on, the Nazi war machine was forced to rely on oil-production facilities located in occupied countries like Hungary and Romania. The Allies, in turn, inaugurated a counter plan to construct bases in Russia that would extend and expand the theater of air operations, putting these distant oil fields within range of American fighters. In the early summer of 1944, the Eighth Air Force completed construction on three Ukrainian airfields—Mirgorod, Piryatin, and Poltava. Once established, these bases were part of a *flying triangle* of bombing raids that would take Horham bombers from England to Russia, then to Italy, over France, and finally, back to England.

The preparation for these missions, part of what was labeled the *Frantic V* or *Operation Frantic* campaign, was extensive. For example, each B-17 carried an extra man, a ground-crew member, as well as mechanical kits and spare parts. If anything happened to the bombers or their escorts so far from their main supply bases, they would have to engineer the fix on their own, so these bombers packed an assortment of tools and supplies. The aircraft were also fitted with a special bomb-bay fuel tank to increase range. In addition to the technological preparation for these extended flights, crew members received special instructions about their expected behavior once they landed in Russia. One member of the combat wing remembered, "We were briefed not to get out of our airplanes in Russia until we had changed from our flying clothes to Class A uniform." Many of the selected aircraft were also "the newer models of our B-17Gs that were bright aluminum and had not been painted a camouflage olive drab color." Crew members received immunizations against Russian viruses as well as language cards and a tutorial in the basic operations at Russian bases. The mission was taking shape as a break in the usual routine of French and German bombing runs, even a bit of adventure, but it was also a raid with great risks. The Germans knew the bombers were coming, and in June, they had attacked Poltava. One hundred tons of Luftwaffe ordnance fell on the base, destroying more than forty B-17s and a primary fuel storage facility. It was a costly loss for the Eighth.

It was in this atmosphere that Henry prepared for his Russian mission. On August 6, the crew was one of thirty-seven selected to fly to Poland. The target was Rahmel and a major aircraft factory. Originally known by its Polish name, Rumia, German occupiers rechristened the city Rahmel. Since 1939, the city had been the site of heavy fighting. After the Nazi takeover of the region, Nazi SS units terrorized the local population of ethnic Poles and Jews. Rahmel was also home to a POW camp for several thousand English and French soldiers. Their forced labor was used to work the nearby Focke-Wulf aircraft-assembly plant. Bombers from Horham hit the plant in force. After their successful drop, part of the group flew on toward Mirgorod, joining a second group including Henry and the rest of the crew. As they landed at the still-damaged Poltava airfield, the airmen got an up-close look at modern war's awesome, destructive power. Base buildings, as well as much of the surrounding community, revealed the impact of the recent German raid. Rubble and ruin were everywhere. One member of the group described the view from above: "As we flew over Poltava, a city of sixty thousand people, we could see into the basement of every building in town." The entire city had been leveled. Henry's recollections were similar. "I didn't see a single building with a roof. The Germans, it seemed, had destroyed everything."

As ground crews, including groups of Russian women, attended their plane after the mission, Henry and Frank Psota walked the short distance from the base into town. They met a pair of local girls who were no doubt enamored with the well-dressed Americans. As the four walked down a main boulevard, a group of young men approached and began yelling at the women. The language barrier prevented Henry and Frank from a perfect understanding of the situation, but the discussion was heated. As the tension escalated, the men assaulted the young women. Henry bore witness to an early version of the tension that would soon dictate the postwar relationship between the world's superpowers. The Americans and the Russians were allies, of course, but the sight of Poltava girls walking through a bombed-out city with two well-fed American fliers in Class As was too much for these locals. Outnumbered, Henry and Frank left the scene unharmed but still shaken by the intensity of the exchange.

The following morning, August 7, Henry witnessed further evidence of the impact of the war on Russia. He watched as a local ground crew loaded bombs into the bay by hand. At Horham, bomb-loading machines and advanced equipment made quick work of the process, but here, crews experienced the strains of war in a direct way. With bombs loaded, the crew took off bound for Trzebina, an oil refinery south of Warsaw. At nearly eleven hours, it would be their second, long mission in a row. With a relatively small squad of P-51 escorts, a bomber wing of more than fifty B-17s dropped 130 tons of Russian-made bombs on the target. As their bomber banked away, Henry looked down and saw nothing but "smoke . . . billows of black, black smoke rising up from the city." With the entire operation planned and executed so far from Horham, the mission proved extremely stressful, and when the exhausted crew landed at Poltava they were, Henry concluded, just happy to be safe.

On their third day, the assault continued, and the crew raided a major airfield near Buzău in southeastern Romania. Buzău was a transportation link, especially for the Black Sea region, and in part due to its vital location, the city witnessed multiple, military invasions dating to the late Middle Ages. Ottoman raiders hit the city in the last decade of the sixteenth century; the Tatars came in the early years of the seventeenth; with Turkish invaders coming a few decades later. Russian Cossacks ravaged the city in the eighteenth century, burning the town and destroying its cathedral. Natural disasters, including a massive cholera epidemic and the black plague, visited the city at the beginning of the nineteenth century, followed by yet another invasion force, this time Greek rebels. Despite this all-star list of disruption and devastation, Buzău persisted, and even with German occupation in WWI, thrived. World War II brought a new level of intense fighting to the community as Soviet and German troops battled for control of the city. The bombers from the Ninety-Fifth were just the latest group to come to this Black Sea city hoping to free the region from Nazi control.

This was not the first time the Ninety-Fifth had conducted operations here. In 1943, an earlier mission took a heavy toll on the Mighty Eighth. Buzău was close to the Ploieşti oil fields, an important refinery of crude oil in the Transylvanian Alps north of Bucharest. The Germans defended the region with major fortifications. Almost exactly one year earlier, August 1, 1943, heavy bombers from bases in North Africa flew toward the oil fields through low mountain passes. Several bombers managed to hit the target, destroying storage tanks and machinery, but the B-17s encountered determined German resistance. Dense flak, heavy machine-gun fire, tenacious anti-aircraft cannons, and swarming, German fighter planes took out many American planes and their crews. More than three hundred crewmen from the Eighth were lost, with 130 wounded. Only thirty-three of the 178 aircraft that took part in the raid survived to fly the next day.

In 1944, thanks to Russian attacks, Ploieşti was
no longer a Nazi bastion of defense, and the Ninety-
Fifth improbably completed its mission without losing
a single aircraft. After a nine-hour flight over
Yugoslavia, Henry and the rest of the Psota crew landed
at an Italian airbase near Foggia, a city on the Adriatic
Sea. Earlier in the war, Benito Mussolini's fascist forces
controlled Foggia. In the early fighting of the war,
Foggia was a critical center for railroad transportation,
but all the action in and around the city had reduced
much of the region to a shell. British forces liberated
the city on October 1, 1943, transforming the city into
a base of operations for the Allied offensive up the
Italian peninsula. Beyond the city's importance in the
battle for control of Italy, the nearby airbase became
a strategic home for the Fifteenth Air Force. From
their new location, American crews launched sorties
north into Germany and westward into southern
France. When Henry arrived in Foggia, he witnessed
the destruction resulting from Allied bombing first
hand. Like Poltava, Foggia was a city broken by war.
Henry had a visceral reaction to his arrival. "The
whole city smelled of death," he remembered. Still,
even amid such destruction, Henry found much to
appreciate about southern Italy. During their four-day
layover, Henry and bombardier William Greene
explored the sights in the ancient city and were even
able to swim and sail in the Gulf of Manfredonia. For

a precious few hours, the war slipped away as Henry bathed in the Italian sun.

On August 12, Henry and the crew flew the final leg of the mission, which also became his last combat run of the war. Escorted by P-51 fighters, B-17s conducted a raid at the Toulouse-Francazal Aérodrome in France. Toulouse, the capital city of France's southern Pyrenees region, was home to a major airfield used by Luftwaffe aircraft, and the Allies wanted to solidify control of the area. Henry remembered that their airplane was a "real dog" and was barely able to keep up with the formation. At one point, the bomber unexpectedly lost altitude, almost crashing into the mountains of Corsica. Despite the trouble, the crew released its bomb load and made it back to Horham in one piece. After parking the plane on its hardstand, the excited crewmembers shot off flares, making it appear as if their wounded plane had exploded. After this pyrotechnic prank, Henry and the rest of the crew celebrated their unbelievable fortune with Italian liquor they had picked up in Foggia. The backslapping got out of hand quickly, and, with the entire crew "two sheets to the wind," the base commander let the men skip the required mission debriefing.

The extended multi-part bombing run gave Henry credit for thirty-two missions and induction into Horham's Lucky Bastard Club. The club, remembered one member of the Ninety-Fifth Bomb Group, honored

Horham's *Lucky Bastard* club.

airmen who completed the required number of missions: a full tour of duty in the Mighty Eighth Air Force. The ceremony followed the same pattern every time. The fortunate crew would dress in their Class A uniforms and assemble in the officers' mess hall. At a head table, draped in a white cloth, the crew was feted with a steak dinner—their only such meal of the war—and fine wine. All the other combat officers gathered in salute and gave the Lucky Bastards a standing ovation. Compared to the drama of the bombing run over Berlin, such an event may seem trivial, but the ceremony was an important milestone and everyone at Horham knew it. These men had survived when so many had not. For Henry, the day was all the more special. At nearly the exact moment of his celebratory dinner, he received his diploma from the University of Michigan.

On August 16, Henry sent a brief twenty-word telegram to his father. It read:

MISSIONS COMPLETED ON MY WAY HOME TELL MOM
EVERYTHING FEELING FINE STOP WRITING GET LOTS
OF STEAKS LOVE HANK BLOCH

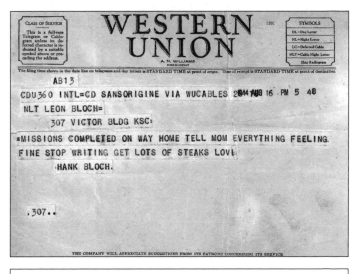

Telegram from Henry to his father, Leon. August 16, 1944.

He packed his belongings in his Horham footlocker and made the necessary arrangements to leave England for good. Less than a month later, Henry stood on the deck of the RMS *Queen Mary*, waiting to put the war behind him.

Like the *Queen Elizabeth* that had brought him to war, the *Queen Mary*, the flagship of the Cunard line, had been transformed into a massive, military-transport vessel. Henry and the rest of the passengers were scheduled to return several days earlier, but the departure of the *Queen Mary* was delayed for the arrival of an important passenger. Henry and the other one thousand homeward-bound troops would be accompanied on this voyage by Sir Winston Churchill, his wife, Mary, and several of his chiefs of staff. Churchill, who was listed pseudonymously on the ship manifest as *Colonel Warden*, was enroute to Halifax, Nova Scotia, and the Second Québec Conference. Code named *Octagon*, the Québec gathering was a high-level, military planning session between the English and American governments. President Franklin Roosevelt was scheduled to meet with Churchill in Québec. There, the two world leaders were to discuss the Lend-Lease program, the future of Germany, and the role of the Royal Navy in the war against the Japanese. The departure delay, Henry remembered, even for someone like Churchill, had significant consequences. He heard a rumor that several wounded soldiers waiting for transport home did not live long enough to make the voyage. On September 5, 1944, the *Queen Mary* finally pulled away from the Gourock pier accompanied by a large convoy of defense vessels. The *Queen Mary* was one of the fastest ocean liners in the world, and, in less than five days, the ship crossed more than three thousand miles of open ocean, landing in Nova Scotia on September 10. After Churchill disembarked, the ship prepared for the last leg of the journey into New York harbor. The next day, September 11, the *Queen Mary* sailed the roughly six hundred miles into American waters.

The multiday voyage gave Henry time to reflect on his experiences in the war. On one hand, the journey itself provided a kind of jovial capstone to the war. Henry recalled with fondness a casual meeting with Mrs. Churchill while strolling the decks. For his part, Frank Psota had a more significant brush with the ship's VIP passengers. Lost, wandering about the large ship, Psota came upon an open door and glanced in hoping to find directions. Instead, the airman found himself in the presence of Prime Minister Churchill. "I passed a room and I looked in, and there he was in his black jacket and a cigar," Frank explained. Psota apologized for the disruption and asked the Prime Minister, "Sir, how do I get out of here without getting shot?" Churchill chuckled and offered guidance, leading Frank to conclude that Churchill was "a charming man. My hero." Frank was not done bumping into famous passengers, as one day, on the way to the cafeteria, he encountered a large man blocking the stairwell. "I poked him in the rear to hurry him along" Frank recalled. "He stopped and turned around and looked at me." It was Joe Louis, army soldier and heavyweight champion of the world. Poised on the step above Frank, the boxer was "like a god looking down." Despite Frank's poking, he described the fighter as "good natured." Henry had his share of fun on the trip back to the States as well. As was his expected custom, when Henry had time to relax, he looked for a card game. He had no trouble finding poker players who, unfortunately, relieved him of all of his cash— less than a hundred dollars—in very short order. There were no more card games on the trip home.

In between these fond memories of bumping into celebrities and cardsharps, Henry contemplated the more profound realities of what he and the crew had just accomplished. He had flown thirty-two missions without a single injury, an amazing achievement in the middle of a war. But Henry knew, even in the moment, that he had been fortunate; perhaps he was a lucky bastard after all. He had, for example, been on a bombing run over the North Sea and saw a neighboring plane burst into flames. Transfixed, he watched out the navigator's window as the damaged aircraft managed to stay aloft long enough for men to get to the open door and parachute out. Henry recognized that in such frigid waters, however, survival was unlikely. One by one he saw men jump out of the burning aircraft into the icy waters. "I knew they were dead men," he recalled. As he watched the crew jump to certain death, he remembered a cold sweat running down his back. Such an ending was almost his. On the bombing raid to the Ploieşti oil fields, Henry left his seat at the navigator's table and walked up to the bombardier's station to get a better view of the bomb drop below. He had been gone for only a few moments when he heard a blast. "When I turned around, a portion of one side of our plane—the side where I had been sitting—was gone." Had fate not intervened at that particular moment, Henry would be dead. Such close calls were all too common for the men that served in B-17s in the skies over Europe. How could the veterans who risked their lives on every flight find peace? That would become a driving question for postwar America.

Experiences like these encouraged a stoicism that shaped Henry's outlook on life. Given the anxiety, severity, and vicious unpredictability of modern, air warfare, a stoic fatalism seems like a reasonable psychological defense mechanism for a young airman. For his part, Henry continues to insist that he did "not do anything special." He never considered himself a hero and spent much of his adult life reticent about the war. Henry, for example, has a number of life-long friends, chief among them Edward T. Matheny, Jr. and Bill Dunn, Sr. This trio regularly played golf and tennis during a close relationship that has stretched over decades. Successful in business, law, and industry, the three friends had something else in common: each served honorably in World War II. But the trio, even

Ed Matheny, Jr., Bill Dunn, Sr., and Henry Bloch.
December 16, 2016. Kansas City.

in their private moments, never discussed their wartime memories until the Kansas City Public Library invited them to speak at an event commemorating the war's seventieth anniversary in March 2015. Despite this reluctance to speak of his experiences, there is little doubt that Henry's time in Europe influenced him in ways both large and small, and that these wartime lessons shaped the way he navigated his own life in the years to come.

HARVARD UNIVERSITY

CAMBRIDGE · MASSACHUSETTS

THIS IS TO CERTIFY THAT

1ST LT HENRY W. BLOCH

has completed the course of
instruction at the

ARMY AIR FORCES STATISTICAL SCHOOL

established by

HEADQUARTERS, ARMY AIR FORCES

given at the

Graduate School of Business Administration
Harvard University

January 27, 1945

_____   _____
Commandant   Civilian Director

Henry's certificate of completion from the Statistical Control program.
January 1945.

Harvard

Henry's homecoming was brief because even though his combat flying was over, his time in the military was not. Not long after his return to the States, in late 1944, as the Ninety-Fifth continued its aerial assaults against German factories and oil fields, Henry began the next segment of his Army Air Force career at the Harvard Business School. In cooperation with the military, Harvard helped design and implement a statistical control program to teach officers a new management strategy. Henry often describes himself as an average student. That he ended up at Harvard seemed a strange quirk of army "wisdom," he says. But the reality is somewhat different than his perception. As a decorated officer with hundreds of hours of combat flight time and a degree in mathematics from the University of Michigan, he was an ideal candidate for the army's new level of administrative command. Just how suited he was for the program became apparent quickly.

Statistical control's intellectual origins and its home on the Harvard campus were the result of a serendipitous synchronicity of ideas, institutions, and people. Before World War II, the Army Air Force organizational structure resembled, as Assistant Secretary of War Robert A. Lovett once remarked, "a bowl of spaghetti." Lovett knew that if the army were to be an effective fighting force, the spaghetti leadership model had to change. Fortunately, as an assistant secretary for war, Lovett was in a position to transform the Army Air Force during its unprecedented wartime growth. Keeping up with the needs of a modern aerial fighting force, Lovett oversaw the expansion of the Army Air Force, including the development and acquisition of large numbers of aircraft for use during the war. For his wartime labors, Lovett received the Distinguished Service Medal and was heralded by President Harry Truman as responsible for "the growth of . . . American airpower which has astonished the world and played such a large part in bringing the war to a speedy and successful conclusion." After World War II ended, Lovett served in several high government offices, first, as the under secretary of state, followed by a stint as the deputy secretary of defense, and finally as the secretary of defense during the Korean War. After his official service ended, Lovett spent much of his later political career as a foreign-policy advisor, described by one scholar as a member of *The Wise*

Men, a group of political insiders who shaped America's international policy during the early decades of the Cold War. These many accomplishments, however, were predicated on his early work with statistical control, which modernized the American military and helped assure Allied victory in World War II.

With the assistance of a close aid, Charles "Tex" Thornton, Lovett incorporated statistics, especially a focus on analytical rigor, into the armed forces. At the beginning of the European conflict, Thornton, just twenty-six, was working as an entry-level statistician in a New Deal housing agency. His fact-based reports brought him to the attention of Lovett, who transferred Thornton to the army to help institutionalize scientific accountability in military planning and decision making. The division they built, *Stat Control*, became the mechanism to bring order to the Armed Forces. As hard as this is to believe for today's readers, before the creation of statistical control, no one was exactly sure how many military personnel were serving in uniform. Nor was it known how many aircraft were available, where spare parts were housed, or where needed mechanics were stationed. In 1939, such ignorance was of little importance to a nation at peace. By 1941, however, knowing such information was critical to basic military objectives.

Stat control began with a simple, albeit extensive, headcount project. Men from the agency were dispatched around the country and to wartime bases around the globe to count aircraft, to complete inventories of men and equipment, and to locate fuel and other available resources. They discovered the expected problems. Bombers in need of replacement parts sat idle at one base while a nearby airfield had a stockpile of the needed equipment. Stat control connected the dots and improved military recording, communication, and productivity. Soon, Thornton's men would do more than tally spare tires. Representatives from Stat Control calculated required bomb loads for various targets, examined fuel consumption rates of different aircraft, and arranged mission objectives to maximize efficiencies. With such information at the ready, Thornton's group did not just transform supply-chain operations, it influenced top-level military planning. Stat control matched demand and supply during wartime, saving billions of dollars in war resources, and helped bring the war to an end faster than even the most optimistic military leaders had hoped or projected. At first glance, improving the warehousing process for a single replacement part might seem insignificant when measured against the complicated action of a combat theater, but look again. Better statistical control meant more planes in the air, more bombs on Berlin, and more American strength pushing against the Nazi war machine. Thornton had, in essence, launched a managerial revolution within the armed services that would have dramatic, postwar implications.

To make stat control work, Thornton recruited a handful of junior faculty—including a young accounting professor, Robert S. McNamara (future head of Ford Motor Company, secretary of defense, and president of the World Bank)—from the Harvard Business School. Thornton's efforts were audacious: he was attempting to persuade America's preeminent military leaders and planners to yield logistical control to a relatively low-ranking outsider. To pull off such a difficult maneuver, Thornton needed a secure and credible base to launch his information gathering operation. Housing Statistical Control at Harvard University gave him the implicit endorsement and prestige he needed to impress military leaders.

Fortunately for Thornton, he approached Harvard at just the right time. The dean of the Business School, Wallace B. Donham, was worried about how his school would survive the war. During World War I, the Harvard Business School nearly collapsed, as students left for the armed forces and faculty took government-service positions in Washington. Donham feared that a repeated student and faculty exodus during World War II not only threatened the short-term viability of the school, but would also have disastrous, long-term consequences. So, when Thornton suggested that Harvard could help create an Army Air Force school to train officers in statistical control, Donham was on board almost immediately.

Donham's decision to affiliate the Business School with a military program fit a broader pattern of institutional support for the American war effort. Under the leadership of President James Bryant Conant, Harvard had long been an active supporter of American military intervention. Harvard scientists worked on military technology; the university created a large army and navy ROTC program; and the school designed an advanced, military curriculum with courses in camouflage design, geology, and radio electronics. Harvard professors invented incendiary grenades, chaff, fiberglass, and sonar. Doctors from Harvard Medical School worked on anti-malarial drugs for tropical combat zones, synthetic blood plasma, and new treatment methods for burns and other combat wounds. Amid this whirlwind of activity, the Business School was largely absent. Thornton's proposal for stat control brought much-needed financial support and a stable supply of students to the Business School, and it also provided Donham with a viable platform to participate in wartime expansion. For his part, Donham was happy to contribute faculty, facilities, and respectability to Thornton's Stat Control program. Both men shared a vision about a future American society based on the power of numbers and facts. Prewar business strategy, certainly as reflected in the state of the American military, was relatively imprecise and arbitrary. Driven by the exigencies of war, Thornton and Donham sought to turn American industrial capitalism into an efficient machine capable of supporting a world power.

Thornton was given unusual latitude and control in building his training program. He got first pick of the top candidates then stationed at the Army Air Force Officer Candidate School. He also insisted that every stat-control officer be a graduate of the Harvard program. The result was a cadre of officers who understood the same analytical language and shared a commitment to the larger goals of the program. This common philosophical foundation was key to the success of stat control. Numbers, after all, do not tell the full story. Thornton trained his officers to recognize the trends and patterns buried in the data and equipped them with the ability to develop policy from what looked like a bundle of loose statistics to outsiders.

In what started as a five-week program before eventually expanding to eight, Harvard faculty offered courses on advanced statistics, predictive theory, and analytical decision making. Officers in the program remained military—drills, rifles, and uniforms stayed—but the focus shifted away from combat preparedness and toward business applications. One of the program's instructional goals was to expose young officers to the nuances of the complicated statistical-control reporting system. Student soldiers also learned about the sometimes byzantine workings of the Army Air Force organizational structure. Such education was always framed around a larger goal of developing analytical skills to increase logistical efficiency, an especially strong expertise among the Harvard faculty. In small classes built around group cohorts, instructors introduced key theories through what was called the *case-study method*. In short order, this learning module became a trademark of all instruction at the Harvard Business School. Unlike previous teaching models, case-study instruction avoided formal lectures and rote memorization. Instead, students participated in an environment of open discussion and experimentation that fostered critical thinking. In one course, for example, officer-students visited regional army offices and training bases, gathered information about their operations, and then came back to the classroom to create order out of shipping manifests, personnel records, and inventories.

Breaking the information into digestible pieces— usually through extensive graphs and charts—was difficult, but once statistics became "readable," they also became more useful. This detail-driven approach created sophisticated, at times mind-numbing, layers of information, but such nuanced tools were necessary to understand an impossibly large and complicated organization like the army. Students who believed in this managerial method of instruction were transformed into missionaries who preached the gospel of statistics throughout the Army Air Force. It was not always smooth. Statistically driven thinking sometimes led to ideas that were too radical for their time. For example, one stat-control officer recommended the elimination of fighter escorts on bomber runs as a cost-saving measure. Regardless of the mathematical merits of the proposition, Air Force leadership could not justify such a callous priority of dollars over lives, and the stat-control officer earned a sharp rebuke from line commanders. On the whole, however, the program produced more hits than misses and transformed field operations throughout the military.

By 1944, the pool of available and qualified stat-control soldiers in the officer candidate school was shrinking, and Thornton opened the program to experienced officers. It did not take long for officers with combat experience to fill Harvard classrooms. The shift in candidates was also reflected in a shift in program emphasis. In the early years, students were exposed to new accounting methods with the intent of matching equipment and people. That is, stat-control officers made sure the Army Air Force had the right number of flight crews and aircraft. Later, students with unique experiences from the field were able to tackle more complicated problems related to supply chains and engineering models. The result was a second wave of students able to solve the structural problems of supply that plagued the army, as well as addressing more fundamental questions about how the army organized its operations.

Given this programmatic change, it makes sense that after his return from Europe, Henry would be enthusiastically admitted into the Harvard training program. His educational background, training scores,

Henry in uniform.

and combat experience made him an ideal candidate. Although at the time of his application, Henry was not exactly sure what happened at Stat Control, he was excited about exposure to the most innovative practices in organizational management. In letters to his family, especially his brothers, Leon and Dick, Henry detailed how much he enjoyed the program. Toward the end of his Horham tour, he wrote, life slowed to a crawl. Long missions and the accompanying stress and strain of combat narrowed his focus. "I was just marking time," he wrote, hoping to get home alive. At Harvard, however, "I don't [think] that anymore." Henry confided to his family, "I'm really getting much more done now than I could if I were in civilian life." He was so taken by his early exposure to stat-control training that he admitted to "spend[ing] my nights . . . reading books and making notes."

For experienced soldiers, the program was an obvious but no less welcome change from combat duty, but few took to the training like Henry. The workload reminded him of his early days in navigator's school with classroom instruction "from 8 to 5 every day" followed by "3 or 4 hours of homework each night." Coursework covered "every part of the organization setup of the Army Air Force" with daily written assignments consisting of "reports about everything." Even with such a heavy load, he wrote, he still managed to spend an additional "hour or two reading books on corporations every day." He joked about leading a monastic life—he hadn't had a date or seen a show in more than two months—but he found the training more rewarding than he imagined. The work, both satisfying and challenging, "gives me a chance to use my head and do a little thinking," he concluded.

Henry's experience in the field informed his efforts in Harvard's classrooms. In a second letter home, Henry described a classroom assignment where he was charged with reorganizing the reporting structure of a combat squadron. In front of his peers and a skeptical professor, he argued for new lines of communication and direct reporting that would improve efficiencies and eliminate possible errors in the field. His presentation also pointed out the possible flaws in his proposal—when he expressed doubt about the real-life application of his reorganization plan, the majority of his classmates were quick to shout down his concerns. Always modest, Henry admitted to his family that he had absolutely no intention of telling General Hap Arnold, commander of the U.S. Army Air Forces, about his plans, but he was pleased with his ability to persuade his faculty and peers.

After completing the statistical-control training program in January 1945, not long after General Douglas MacArthur was placed in command of all American ground troops, Henry received orders to report to Walker Army Air Field. Walker Field, today abandoned, was the army's primary B-29 Superfortress training base. Walker was also home to the Fifty-Eighth Bomb Wing, the first combat wing engaged in the long-range bombing of Japan. Located outside the small Kansas town of Hays—closer to his Kansas City home than he had been since he joined the army—the base, hot and dusty in the summer and cold and drafty in the winter, had humble beginnings. But, by the time of Henry's arrival, Walker Field was one of the most important training centers for the entire air force. For Henry, the base would also provide a platform to use his natural abilities in mathematics and his newly acquired skills in statistics to great effect.

Walker Field had been constructed in 1942 as part of the accelerated military buildup following the Japanese attack on Pearl Harbor. The base was originally built for just one thousand soldiers, with the most basic of services and three large but simple runways. Supplies were short, so most of the early buildings were wood and tarpaper, just like what Henry had grown accustomed to in San Antonio. In the base's second year, 1943, Walker was designated home to the 503rd Bombardment Squadron, expanding with the addition of a signal corps detachment, medical unit, ordnance corps, weather squadron, quartermaster company, and base headquarters. Walker continued to grow, eventually becoming a processing center. With the added personnel, Walker Field soon resembled a more traditional military base with a gymnasium, theater, officers' club, and post exchange.

What the base looked like, however, was less important than what the base did. In the middle of 1943, the first of the B-29s arrived, and throughout the rest of the war, Walker served as the training ground for the Seventeenth Bombardment Operational Training Wing. Problems of growth became apparent almost immediately. Originally intended for a small cohort of soldiers with one hangar, Walker was laid out with just one bombing range. With the sky over the base crowded with bombers, the airfield became dangerous for young officers learning their craft. As a short-term solution, army officials allowed Walker pilots to practice at nearby ranges, but such policy only contributed to congestion at other bases. Walker Air Base acquired additional acreage, mostly from local farmers, for bombing practice, but even this expansion proved inadequate, as the arrival of additional bombers continued to strain base resources. The base was reorganized in spring 1944 with the goal of creating a complete bombardment-training center capable of preparing aircrews and aircraft for combat in two different theaters of engagement. When Henry arrived at the airfield in 1945, the base included nearly 3,000 enlisted men and 530 officers in training, with a permanent staff of 235 officers, 1,800 enlisted men, and 660 civilians. The logistics of managing the base, while keeping waves of aircraft in the sky and everyone safe, was an incredible challenge—but it was exactly the kind of problem Tex Thornton built Statistical Control to handle.

Henry arrived at Walker as a personnel officer, a bland title that belies its significance. He joked that all he did was "sign the occasional weekend pass to town," when, in truth, to Henry fell the task of managing the operations of much of the base, work that directly engaged the lessons of efficient management he studied at Harvard. In a letter to his father, Henry described his work assignments. Typical of many of the officers to emerge from stat-control training, Henry admitted that he crammed "about 18 hours of work" into a single eight-hour shift. Thornton pushed his students to work long days without interruption; Henry's experiences were no exception. His job, he noted, "is one of . . . the most important ones on the field" and suited "perfectly to my taste." It may not sound exciting, he admitted; it is, after all "simply accounting, personnel accounting," but "I think it is wonderful . . . [and] out here things are better than ever."

"To give you some idea of the importance of it," he continued, "the schedules [I] make up determine the output of the Bomb Groups." If he did his job correctly, the base was marked with "lots of flying" and his boss, "a Major whose office is in another building," would happily make lieutenant colonel. Even a small mistake meant "little flying" and the "General down on [my] head."

Henry's job had little room for advancement or promotion, but he did not care. "I'm extremely satisfied . . . mainly because I have a job that offers a real test for my ability." Early in his appointment, he made a number of significant operational changes that altered base workflow, and he did so with an influence far above that of most first lieutenants. As he explained to his father, "My days are spent in conferences with all the biggest men on the field." He asked for forgiveness if such comments came off as boasting: "I don't want this to sound in any way like conceit," but the work he was doing was significant to the base and to the war effort. "Probably the nicest part about it," he continued, "is the fact that my work is so important that the Colonels have to ask me favors, and I can tell them exactly what I want done." He explained that he had "control over 2,500 men, two private phones with different lines, a secretary, five WACs, [an] E.M., [and] a jeep with driver." Henry's personnel management position was an appointment carved straight from the Stat Control playbook. A single officer, trained in the newest techniques of statistical management, could revolutionize operations on a massive air base.

After the excitement of a B-17, Henry wasn't sure that Walker Army Air Field would be a good fit. "I didn't think I'd like it when I began," he wrote, but it turned out better than he anticipated. He did not miss combat, and, unexpectedly, he found life in western Kansas to his liking. In one letter home he noted, "The weather has turned nice, which means lots of tennis, golf, and swimming." That week alone, he attended "a party, two picnics," and found "there's plenty to keep me busy." More significant than the changes to his social calendar was the recognition that at Walker, Henry found an unexpected aptitude for business management.

How this training would translate into an America transformed by war, however, remained an open question. Indeed, uncertainty appeared to characterize much of American life in the spring of 1945. The tide of war had swung toward the Allies, but the fighting, including the brutal island hopping of the Pacific theater, continued. The American economy was growing, but memories of the Depression—and fears of its return—were still on the minds of many citizens. Perhaps most significant, on April 12, while Henry continued his assignment at Walker Air Field, President Franklin Roosevelt died. The war had taken a noticeable toll on the president, and his friends encouraged him to rest and recover. He traveled to Warm Springs, Georgia, a health spa familiar to the Roosevelt family, where surrounded by his closest family and aides, he suffered a massive cerebral hemorrhage. For many Americans, FDR was the only president they knew, and worry about the management of the war effort, international politics, and the shape of postwar society clouded the nation's future. As the nation moved into an anxious summer, Henry hoped that his management acumen—a combination of skills picked up in the training fields of the Texas plains, the flak-filled skies over Germany, and the classrooms of Harvard—would help him chart a new course in postwar America.

MILITARY RECORD AND REPORT OF SEPARATION
CERTIFICATE OF SERVICE

1. LAST NAME - FIRST NAME - MIDDLE INITIAL	2. ARMY SERIAL NUMBER	3. ADS. GRADE	4. ARM OR SERVICE	5. COMPONENT
BLOCH HENRY W	0 707 764	1st Lt	AC	AUS

6. ORGANIZATION	7. DATE OF RELIEF FROM ACTIVE DUTY	8. PLACE OF SEPARATION
412 Sq 95 B Gp ETO	22 July 1945	Jefferson Barracks Missouri

9. PERMANENT ADDRESS FOR MAILING PURPOSES	10. DATE OF BIRTH	11. PLACE OF BIRTH
414 W 58th Street Kansas City Missouri	30 July 1922	Kansas City Missouri

12. ADDRESS FROM WHICH EMPLOYMENT WILL BE SOUGHT	13. COLOR EYES	14. COLOR HAIR	15. HEIGHT	16. WEIGHT	17. NO. OF DEPENDENTS
Kansas City Missouri	Grey	Brown	5'8"	157 lbs.	0

18. RACE				19. MARITAL STATUS			20. U.S.CITIZEN		21. CIVILIAN OCCUPATION AND NO.
WHITE	NEGRO	OTHER (specify)	SINGLE	MARRIED	OTHER (specify)	YES	NO	
X			X			X		Student College X-02

MILITARY HISTORY

SELECTIVE SERVICE DATA	22. REGISTERED	23. LOCAL S. S. BOARD NUMBER	24. COUNTY AND STATE	25. HOME ADDRESS AT TIME OF ENTRY OR ACTIVE DUTY
	YES NO X			Kansas City Missouri

26. DATE OF ENTRY ON ACTIVE DUTY	27. MILITARY OCCUPATIONAL SPECIALTY AND NO.	
15 Jan 1944	Navigator 1034	APPLICATION FOR READJUSTMENT ALLOWANCE PUBLIC LAW #346 ...DE THROUGH ...TATE MISSOURI ...DATE SEP 7 1945

28. BATTLES AND CAMPAIGNS
Air Offensive Europe Normandy Northern France

29. DECORATIONS AND CITATIONS
Air Medal with 3 Oak Leaf Clusters EAME with 3 Bronze Stars

30. WOUNDS RECEIVED IN ACTION
None

31. SERVICE SCHOOLS ATTENDED	32. SERVICE OUTSIDE CONTINENTAL U. S. AND RETURN		
	DATE OF DEPARTURE	DESTINATION	DATE OF ARRIVAL
Advanced Navigator Training Hondo Texas	25 Mar 1944	ETO	9 Apr 1944

33. REASON AND AUTHORITY FOR SEPARATION			
Demobilization RR 1-5 SO 195 Par 4 Hq WAAF Walker Kansas 14 July 1945	15 Sept 1944	USA	25 Sept 1944

34. CURRENT TOUR OF ACTIVE DUTY						35.	EDUCATION (years)		
CONTINENTAL SERVICE			FOREIGN SERVICE				GRAMMAR SCHOOL	HIGH SCHOOL	COLLEGE
YEARS	MONTHS	DAYS	YEARS	MONTHS	DAYS				
1	0	7	0	6	0		8	4	4

INSURANCE NOTICE

IMPORTANT IF PREMIUM IS NOT PAID WHEN DUE OR WITHIN THIRTY-ONE DAYS THEREAFTER, INSURANCE WILL LAPSE. MAKE CHECKS OR MONEY ORDERS PAYABLE TO THE TREASURER OF THE U. S. AND FORWARD TO COLLECTIONS SUBDIVISION, VETERANS ADMINISTRATION, WASHINGTON 25, D. C.

36. KIND OF INSURANCE			37. HOW PAID		38. Effective Date of Allotment Discontinuance	39. Date of Next Premium Due (one month after 38)	40. PREMIUM DUE EACH MONTH	41. INTENTION OF VETERAN TO		
Nat. Serv.	U.S. Govt.	None	Allotment	Direct to V.A.				Continue	Continue only	Discontinue
X			X		July 1945	Aug 1945	* 6.50	X	*	

42.	RIGHT THUMB PRINT	43. REMARKS (This space for completion of above items or entry of other items specified in W. D. Directives)
		LAPEL BUTTON ISSUED EM CADET from 22 Mar 1943 to 14 Jan 1944

44. SIGNATURE OF OFFICER BEING SEPARATED	45. PERSONNEL OFFICER (Type name, grade and organization - signature)
Henry W Bloch	Thomas C. Henry THOMAS C HENRY 1st Lt QMC Asst Adjutant

WD AGO FORM 53-98
1 November 1944

This form supersedes all previous editions of WD AGO Forms 53 and 280 for officers entitled to a Certificate of Service, which will not be used after receipt of this revision.

Military discharge paperwork, July 1945.

Business

In the middle of an unusually warm summer at Walker Air Base, six weeks shy of the end of World War II, First Lieutenant Henry Bloch was ordered to appear at the Separation Center, Jefferson Barracks, St. Louis, Missouri. He made the trek east across his home state of Missouri where, on July 22, 1945, he was officially and honorably discharged from the United States Army Air Force. The young man who made his way back to Kansas City bore little resemblance to the nervous teenager who left for Michigan several years earlier, but like millions of other returning soldiers, he still faced the challenge of transitioning back into civilian life.

Henry moved back in with his parents and almost immediately began looking for work. In a difficult employment market flooded with veterans, he landed a position as a temporary bookkeeper with H.O. Peet, a local brokerage firm. After a short time with the company, Henry passed the securities examination and became a stockbroker. It seemed like a promising beginning. H.O. Peet was a thriving company with a considerable portfolio and a strong presence in the community. Plus, with Henry's work habits and skill set, he was no doubt destined for a quick move up the company hierarchy. The only snag—and it was a big one—was that Henry hated it. He did not like the work, which he found hollow, or the atmosphere. As he explained to his father in a moment of exasperation, "I'm not getting anywhere . . . . All I do is phone clients and watch stocks go across the ticker tape." Given all that Henry recently experienced, it is not surprising that he would want a career with more meaning, nor is it unexpected that, as he tried to craft a path forward, his army training would once again become influential.

Henry's long months of flight school honed a disciplined work ethic, just as his combat experiences deepened his appreciation for teamwork and cooperation. It was during statistical-control training that he had found an application for these traits. During extended lunch breaks at that time, Henry would often forgo eating in favor of perusing the stacks at Baker Library, the main repository for the Harvard University School of Business. He was searching for new ideas, looking to chart a career path for after the war. It was on one of these noontime adventures that he stumbled across a transcript of a speech given by Sumner H. Slichter, a Harvard professor of economics and the chief labor economist in 1940s America. The speech,

"Enterprise in Postwar America," was delivered to the National Association of Investment Companies in early 1943. As Henry skimmed the speech, he became interested in Slichter's ideas and began to read with more focus. While many prominent economists, such as Gunnar Myrdal, predicted that without the guarantee of government war spending, the American economy would enter a period of steep decline, Slichter argued the near reverse. Henry shared that opinion, and this discovery in the library confirmed his plans for life after the war.

That Henry was so captivated by Slichter's work is, perhaps, not as accidental as it might seem. Although he is not a household name today, Slichter was one of the most accomplished economists in America. A native of Wisconsin with an advanced degree from the University of Chicago, he held an endowed position at Harvard, was past president of the American Economic Association, and wrote the standard economics textbook of the period, *Modern Economic Society*. In addition to his academic work, Slichter reached a wide audience with frequent commentary in popular outlets like *Harper's Magazine*.

In the 1930s, Slichter was skeptical about President Roosevelt's New Deal and its promise of full employment. But as the war drew to a close, he did not share in the fear of a return to Depression-era America. Indeed, Slichter's vision was considerably brighter. In returning veterans, he saw not the potentially unemployed but a large force of skilled workers able to contribute to a new society. He also forecast that this new American class of workers would become avid consumers, buying durable goods long out of reach because of wartime limitations. In this "catch-up economy," consumer demand would drive long-term growth. He predicted that the transition from war production to the domestic consumer market would be smoother than many proposed and that increased demand for housing and automobiles would boost the overall economy.

The idea that most captivated Henry was Slichter's insistence that the economic conditions of postwar America provided the ideal environment for small investors to become entrepreneurs. Slichter argued that the next generation of American business leaders would come from a new class of investors capable of

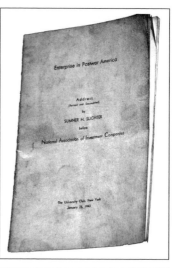

Cover of *Enterprise in Postwar America*, by Sumner H. Slichter.

providing services that aided the growth of the larger economy. He did not argue against individual benefit, but he applauded investment that improved society. Making a case for investors to see value in the greater good, Slichter's work prefigured the benefits of creative entrepreneurs who started small and built both social and economic capital. That day in Boston, in Harvard's Baker Library, Henry made plans for a company that could link investors and their capital with prospective business owners who wanted to build new enterprises. It would be the embodiment of Slichter's ideal. Henry would help innovative citizens realize their potential by providing access to much-needed capital. Investors would see a positive return, just as the larger economy grew through job creation.

Not long after finding the Slichter speech transcript, Henry wrote a series of letters to his two brothers, Dick and Leon Jr., sketching out the rough outline of his idea. "People all over the country will want to start businesses and in doing so will need a certain amount of capital," he began. "At the same time, others will have capital that they want to invest." Henry then put himself in the middle of the equation. "Our idea is to combine these needs. The person who wants to start a business . . . will come to see us, at which time we will tell him that if he will incorporate we will get him the money. We do everything for him, the incorporating, the issuing of stocks and their sale to people who wish to find a good investment." As Henry continued to fill in the details of the new business, he repeatedly fell back on lessons from the war. Combat taught Henry the importance of teamwork, trust, and cooperation. Now he passed that imperative to his brothers. "The most important thing is our reputation," he noted. "Investors must have confidence in us."

As they debated various options to pursue, it soon became clear that the business of the Bloch brothers, to paraphrase Calvin Coolidge, would be business. The statistical-control program illustrated the immense value of numbers, and Henry intended to make use of that training in the private sector. He emphasized this theme in additional letters to his brothers. "You've heard the saying that everything in the universe is based on mathematics," Henry explained. It may sound impractical, he admitted, but "everything that we do should have behind it some sort of equation even if only philosophically." It was not numbers alone, of course, but how they could be used. As he concluded succinctly, "Charts and graphs will be important to us and may point out trends." Here, Henry was speaking the language of statistical control. Officers in the program used data to reveal patterns and make predictions about future behavior. It was this exact skill that made stat control so critical to military operations. At Harvard, Henry's classroom exercises relied on multiple data points to create an effective long-term military operations strategy, to

ARMY AIR FORCES
STATISTICAL SCHOOL
HARVARD UNIVERSITY
BOSTON. MASSACHUSETTS

Dec. 29, 1944

Dear Jim,

As you asked, the following are attempts at answering your 46 questions. No references will be made to either yours or Dickie's letters because I haven't read any of them carefully. First let me say that I'm sure you'll think my ideas radical, no doubt they are — but if it's *my* ideas you want then that's what you'll get. I also want to say that they are extremely personal, and so may not be for the best good of you and Dickie — but they do constitute the lines of thought I have on the subject which are *very* definite! Enough said. Sorry I don't have a typewriter.

1. There are 45 other questions to be answered, so if you don't mind I'll move along. I hope this voices your feelings to.

2. Only small things like really settling down to hard work, and matters pertaining to business experience that we must learn in time.

3. Generally speaking, the financing of new businesses. Considering first the natural

Letter from Henry to his brothers about starting a business, written while he was at stat-control training at Harvard. December 29, 1944.

understand the constantly changing field of battle, and to improve battle outcomes with a new emphasis on efficiency. At Walker Air Field, he put such instruction into practice to help manage a critically important bomber base. After the war, he hoped, this same methodology would become the foundation for a business built for the postwar economy.

One more lesson from the military colored Henry's plans for after the war. His experience moving from a young trainee to a decorated combat veteran exposed him to the many ways that the federal government was involved in the war effort. In 1939, the United States faced the challenge of building a fighting force capable of waging war on two sides of the globe, but it was also necessary to create a massive federal structure to manage the economy and direct the administration of the war effort. To a generation of Americans who came of age in the laissez-faire 1920s, the amount of change in the federal government was nearly impossible to fathom; during the war, the government became involved in nearly every aspect of public life. The federal government set prices, determined labor contracts, controlled supply chains, and dictated the management structure of entire industries. As the war began to wind down, many critics pushed for a return to prewar conditions. Long concerned with concentrations of authority, some Americans pushed to dismantle the enlarged bureaucratic apparatus used to organize the war effort. Henry, however, knew that such a position was untenable. The changes in American life were too significant to permit a retreat to an earlier age. In postwar America, the federal government would be the primary engine of growth and development in society. With a keen understanding of the nation's new financial structure, Henry emphasized to his brothers how their new enterprise must create cooperative relationships between business and government. If the Bloch brothers could aid "the rise of the corporation in our economy" and find a way to manage the flow of capital between "corporations [and] the federal government and our national economy," he wrote, they had a shot at real success.

As Henry and his brother Leon discovered, however, success proved elusive. Their first challenge was a shortage of start-up capital. Henry's military contacts were unable to offer assistance, nor did a 1946 return trip to Harvard and Slichter provide much encouragement. Henry hoped Slichter would approve the brothers' fifty-page business plan. Instead, after thanking Henry and his brother Leon for their visit, the economics professor told them that their venture, like most postwar business efforts, would probably fail. The brothers then turned to Kate Wollman—the same side of the family that paid Henry's tuition at the University of Michigan—but this, too, came up short. Instead of the $50,000 in operating capital the brothers requested as a gift, Wollman provided a $5,000 loan. She then went one step further, requiring their father to sign the note. Disappointed but undeterred, Henry and Leon Jr. accepted the loan, and with their $50 a month G.I. stipend, they opened an account for their infant business. Focusing on Kansas City, the community they knew best, Henry and Leon Jr. created United Business Company in 1946, a service-orientated storefront that offered a wide range of options— bookkeeping, advertising, accounting, incorporation, window decorating, to name a few—to new businesses. After much planning and preparation, the Bloch brothers had finally started their careers.

Despite the excitement and enthusiasm that comes with any new venture, the early returns for United Business were bleak. After one particularly difficult stretch, Henry admitted, "We had nothing to show for our effort. Not a single client, not a single prospect. Zero!" They tried cold calls; they knocked on doors, but finding clients was a challenge. After a survey of this less-than-promising landscape, Leon Jr. left the struggling venture and returned to law school, hoping for a more stable and productive career. From virtually every perspective, it was a decision that made perfect sense—but not to Henry. He never considered quitting. Perhaps here was a final consequence of his war experiences: Henry was no longer afraid.

Early in his tour, as he recounted decades later, every mission was a source of great stress. Even on the most routine mission, Henry noted, "We saw planes going down, a few parachutes would pop here and there, but most of those men were dead.... There was death everywhere." His body responded with the same reaction. "As I watched the world from the windows of the navigator compartment, an icy sweat would run down my back each and every time ... I would see all these people dying and knew that it was soon my turn. I was just a young kid, fresh out of school," he continued. "I didn't know much, but I knew I didn't want to die."

As he became more seasoned, however, he stopped worrying. Henry could not explain how or why the transition occurred. Flying over Germany's flak-filled skies remained as intense as ever, but about midway through the war, he adopted a new perspective: "If I die, I die." This radical acceptance stemmed from a firm belief in his contribution to the greater good. Henry later acknowledged that if his plane were "shot down, I would die fighting for my country ... and that was OK." Once he claimed ownership of this new outlook, he was able to reduce the stress of combat flying and became a better and more focused soldier. When applied to his postwar business ventures, these same experiences gave Henry an unusual perspective on risk. He did not become reckless, but he recognized the futility of worry. Even more significant, he was no longer afraid to fail. He was not the same shy young man who, reluctant to leave his hometown, chose a college only a few blocks from his boyhood home. That man was transformed in the skies over Europe. He became a self-proclaimed fatalist during the war. Taken to absurd extremes, fatalism can lead to disengagement and a debilitating level of pessimism. For Henry, this outlook took on a pragmatic, combat-hardened form. He survived the war; he could certainly endure a little rejection. Henry started his business career in Kansas City with an understanding that failure did not define him. Freed from fear, he became a determined entrepreneur. The results would be impressive.

With Leon Jr. out, Henry was on his own. By necessity, he paired the list of services down from fifty to just one—bookkeeping. Henry continued to market himself throughout the city, but customers were in short supply. Each prospective client asked for references, but without any accounts, quality references were scarce. He would catch the occasional break—a burger stand or small storefront would sign on, but it was a particularly hard slog.

In a now familiar pattern, however, Henry persisted. He slowly built a customer base to the point where he needed assistance. In search of a partner, he turned to his brother Dick. The two brothers invested a great deal of time and even more capital into their young enterprise, and although the lean years persisted—in 1947, the net income of their enterprise was less than $350—their company was growing, and the business plan Henry originally sketched out on Army Air Force letterhead several years earlier began

to pay dividends. These early returns were especially welcome, as in the summer of 1951 Henry married the former Marion Helzberg, his life partner for the next six decades. It was one thing to live with his parents, trying to make rent, when Henry was single, but now with Marion, and soon four children— Bob, Tom, Mary Jo, and Liz—to support, he dou-

Henry and Marion's wedding photograph, June 16, 1951.

bled his efforts to make his young business a success.

The brothers charged fifteen dollars a month for bookkeeping, a service that also included preparation of the client's income-tax returns. Soon it was the tax service, not the primary task of bookkeeping, that attracted customers. By 1955, preparing tax returns at five dollars each, the company made more than $20,000. Later that same year, the two brothers dropped the original United Business name, consolidated their services, and formed H&R Block. The next year, 1956, the company branched into New York. In 1957, they expanded their office network nationally.

I Am Doing My Own

INCOME TAX!

Give US all your tax worries! In all probability, we can save you much more than our nominal charge when we prepare your tax returns. Our service is accurate, quick and complete!

$**5**^{00} FEDERAL AND STATE

OPEN
Weekdays
8 A. M. to
9 P. M.
Sat. &
Sun.
8 A. M. to
9 P. M.

We also offer a COMPLETE BOOKKEEPING SERVICE that includes:
● Double Entry Books Kept Up-to-Date
● Preparation of All Tax Returns
● Financial Statements

This Complete Service Only......$8.33 Monthly
K. C.'s LARGEST ACCOUNTING SERVICE

UNITED BUSINESS CO.
3937 MAIN
OPEN Weekdays 8 A. M. to
9 P. M. Sat. & Sun. 8 A. M.
NO APPOINT-
MENT NECESSARY
JE. 6400

First advertisement for United Business Company, January 1955.

From this origin, the success story of H&R Block is well-traveled ground. In 1967, H&R Block had more than fifteen hundred offices in nearly one thousand cities across America. The company continued to grow, employing more than one hundred thousand tax professionals in ten thousand locations worldwide. Diversification followed in the 1970s and 1980s with acquisitions of temporary labor companies, computer information services, and a legal services management firm. In 1991, tax-preparation services at H&R Block accounted for more than $700 million in revenue. A $10,000 investment in the company in 1962, the year the company went public, returned more than $12 million three decades later. By the end of the 1990s, the company built its annual revenues to $1.3 billion.

There is little need to continue this business overview here as the more recent history of the company continued this upward trajectory, but often lost in the story of one of America's most successful entrepreneurs is how the war shaped Henry and his namesake company. As Henry admitted on several occasions, "There would be no H&R Block without World War II." Such sentiment means more than perhaps even Henry recognizes. Statistical-control training and his management responsibilities at Walker Air Field contributed in clear and direct ways to Henry's business acumen, but so too did his varied experiences at Hondo and Horham, Berlin and Poltava. The army instilled an appreciation for the value of camaraderie and loyalty, just as it provided invaluable training in leadership and innovation. That combat changes those who experience it is an all-too-easy cliché, but for Henry, fighting in the war altered his views on risk and failure. Perhaps above all else, the war showed Henry that the best things in life are worth the risks they demand. In an alternative scenario, he might have served in a different theater, or perhaps in a less dangerous capacity, during the war. Returning to Kansas City with a more conservative and less fatalistic outlook, this Henry might have been comfortable continuing to work as a stock broker, settling into a pleasant if unremarkable suburban life. There is nothing wrong with those choices, of course, but for the Henry Bloch who faithfully navigated more than thirty missions—the same young officer who came to terms with the possibility of giving his life over the skies of Europe—there was no interest in settling for a career of comfort or convenience. He knew he was meant for something more.

Epilogue

O n June 30, 2016, Henry Bloch walked into Kansas City's Union Station, the same city landmark he entered almost eight decades earlier to catch a train bound for the University of Michigan. This time he gathered at the station not for the train but for a celebration to rededicate the Henry Wollman Bloch Fountain. Even in a city filled with noted water features, the large Bloch Fountain continues to dazzle visitors. The fountain was originally unveiled in 2001 to mark Henry's retirement as chairman of the board of H&R Block. Now the refurbished and renovated fountain, a gift from the company foundation, would once again draw crowds to the site. The ceremony included key leaders from city government, as well as representatives of Kansas City's civic and business élite. Press photographers and television crews gathered nearby as a city official led the crowd in a countdown that ended with the fountain once again shooting spray into a cloudless sky. Henry, one month shy of turning ninety-four, gave a brief speech thanking the

Henry Wollman Bloch Fountain with Liberty Memorial in the background.

gathered guests for attending and reminding everyone
of his deep appreciation for the city. Afterward, he
made his way through the crowd shaking hands with
old friends and new acquaintances alike.

Henry is well accustomed to such events. He has
spent much of his adult life giving back to the city.
He is a frequent guest at ribbon cuttings and meet-
and-greets all over the metropolitan region. To tour
his downtown office is to see evidence of a life
dedicated to philanthropy. Countless civic awards,
honorary degrees, and gifts of thanks crowd his office
walls and bookshelves. Kansas City's principal art
museum, medical complex, and university—the
Nelson-Atkins Museum of Art, St. Luke's Hospital,
and the University of Missouri-Kansas City—have
received tens of millions in support and endowment

funds from the Bloch family. The fountain unveiling stands as only the latest reminder of Henry's place in the community.

But on this day, the fountain meant something more. When Henry first left home, he gazed out the windows of Union Station, over the open land where his fountain now stands, his eye trailing up the hillside of the Liberty Memorial. The memorial, evidence of the kind of civic pride that would define Henry's life, was built to commemorate the sacrifice of millions who lost their lives in a conflict so horrific that contemporary observers labeled it "the war to end all wars." That a monument could stand as a dedication to peace was a nice sentiment, but just a generation later the world would once again descend into chaos. In 1939, Henry had no way of knowing how this conflagration would change his life, but on this summer day, the fountain, located directly between Union Station and Liberty Memorial, gave him a rare opportunity for pause. The fountain has a series of circular jets that cascade water upward to great heights. The choreography produces a grand effect, but the fountain also includes an outer ring of calm, shallow water. This architecture permits visitors to stand before the display and capture a view that includes the reflection of the station and the memorial encompassed into a single frame.

At the fountain rededication, Henry glanced at the memorial, thinking across the decades, and drifted back to the war years that shaped not only his life but also those of the millions who served during World War II. For the large cohort of Americans too young to have experienced the war, the members of the Greatest Generation hold a special place in the American memory. These Americans helped defeat the scourge abroad, just as they also created a dynamic postwar American economy. Henry did his part in both winning the war and the peace that followed, but he did not do so alone. Just as the success of his B-17 needed a full crew of dedicated soldiers, the prosperity of postwar America relied on contributions from myriad members of American society.

Henry steadfastly refuses the idea that he is special. Instead he holds to the belief that, like the rest of America during that time of peril, he was "just doing his job." This sentiment is by no means limited to Henry, as many members of that generation of Americans express humility in the face of praise. Their refusal to accept individual accolades does not diminish their collective accomplishments. On the contrary, it highlights a commitment to a larger purpose, a dedication to a greater good beyond the reach of any one individual.

Henry learned hard lessons about the capricious nature of death during wartime. That experience,

John Herron and Henry Bloch examine Henry's flight jacket. August 4, 2016.

which could easily have left him unmoored and adrift, propelled him beyond the war with a sense of purpose. He would not settle for a comfortable but unsatisfying career and was undaunted by the long odds of succeeding at his own business. Henry often chalks up his business success to luck. He cites fortunate changes in federal tax policy, a well-timed advertising campaign, or the contributions of his brother, Dick. Rather than false modesty, these claims are his sincere beliefs. Of course, a more sober assessment of his business success prioritizes more traditional ingredients—hard work, savvy decision-making, and shrewd business acumen—over simple good fortune. To look at the role of luck more seriously, however, it becomes apparent that Henry's claims about his career in business are at least partially true. He was lucky to survive his tour of duty, and he no doubt owes a debt to those who did not. His response is to downplay his personal experiences and to share the credit with all who served.

During the many hours of interviews required for this project, Henry spoke often of the larger story of the war. His interest in Doolittle's raid on Tokyo, famous dogfights over Germany, and the island fighting in the Pacific emerged clearly. He frequently shared news clippings and press reports about anniversaries of major battles or memorials to decorated soldiers. Once again, the common theme in each of his stories is to highlight the achievement of well-known military figures, while glossing over his role in the very same conflict. It is worth repeating that Henry's business empire was made possible by the experience of war. It was First Lieutenant Henry W. Bloch who became the chairman of the board—the very same humble young man sitting at the train station, wondering what the world had in store.

Illustrations

and William Fenley. Front row: Henry Bloch, William Greene, Frank Psota, and Warren Kalbacher. Image courtesy of the Bloch family.

Pg. 75   Drawing of Psota flight crew. Image courtesy of the Bloch family.

Pg. 84   Horham navigators in early morning briefing meeting. Image courtesy of Michael Darter and Gerald Grove, 95th Bomb Group Memorials Foundation.

Pg. 89   B-17s ready for takeoff. Image courtesy of Michael Darter and Gerald Grove, 95th Bomb Group Memorials Foundation.

Pg. 90   The control tower at Horham. Image courtesy of Michael Darter and Gerald Grove, 95th Bomb Group Memorials Foundation.

Pg. 92   Heavy bombers from the Ninety-Fifth heading toward Germany. Image courtesy of Michael Darter and Gerald Grove, 95th Bomb Group Memorials Foundation.

Pg. 95   B-17 encountering Axis flak, December 16, 1943. Image courtesy of the American Air Museum in Britain. Object #UPL 19449. Original image from National Archives Record Management, ref# FH-3A19513-E26957AC.

Pg. 97   Bomb impact on German targets. Image courtesy of the Library of Congress Prints & Photographs Division.

Pg. 98   Flight crew debriefing after mission, Horham. Image courtesy of Michael Darter and Gerald Grove, 95th Bomb Group Memorials Foundation.

Pg. 100   A sample mission report from 1944. Flight crews filed reports on weather, enemy activity, and effectiveness of attack after each bombing mission. Flight mission records are available from the National Archives and Records Administration (NARA). See Record Group 18, Combat Mission Reports, 95th BG (H) Mission Folders, 1943-1945, National Archives and Records Administration, Silver Springs, Maryland.

Pg. 103   B-17s line up for takeoff, n.d. Image courtesy of the Library of Congress Prints & Photographs Division.

Pg. 105   Navigator at work in B-17. Image courtesy of Michael Darter and Gerald Grove, 95th Bomb Group Memorials Foundation.

Pg. 106   B-17 dropping bomb load on Nürnberg, Germany, 1944. Image courtesy of the Library of Congress Prints & Photographs Division.

Pg. 113   Mission records illustrate the position of each B-17 in the attack formation (LeMay combat box). The Psota plane is at the bottom left. See Record Group 18, Combat Mission Reports, 95th BG (H) Mission Folders, 1943-1945, National Archives and Records Administration, Silver Springs, Maryland.

Pg. 114   B-17 in flight. Image courtesy of the Library of Congress Prints & Photographs Division.

Pg. 123   Horham's *Lucky Bastard* club. Image courtesy of Michael Darter and Gerald Grove, 95th Bomb Group Memorials Foundation.

Pg. 124   Telegram from Henry to this father, Leon. August 16, 1944. Letter courtesy of the Bloch family.

Pg. 129   Ed Matheny, Jr., Bill Dunn, Sr., and Henry Bloch. December 16, 2016. Kansas City. Image courtesy of David Miles.

Further Reading

Prologue

1. On the history of the memorial, see "Liberty Memorial," a National Historic Landmark Summary Listing for the National Register of Historic Places. The application for landmark status and the summary report, both available online from the National Park Service, provide information about the history and architecture of the memorial and the surrounding grounds. When the World War I Museum was reopened in the fall of 2006, several major newspapers covered the event. As one example see Mark Yost, "Why Kansas City," *Wall Street Journal*, November 29, 2006. See also James M. Mayo, *War Memorials as Political Landscape: The American Experience and Beyond* (Greenwood, CT.: Praeger, 1988) and Derek Donovan, *Lest the Ages Forget: Kansas City's Liberty Memorial* (Kansas City: Kansas City Star Books, 2001).

Beginnings

1. For biographical information on Henry Wollman Bloch, see Thomas M. Bloch, *Many Happy Returns: The Story of Henry Bloch, America's Tax Man* (Hoboken, N.J.: John Wiley & Sons, 2010). Written by Henry's son, Tom, *Many Happy Returns* remains the best single source on Henry Bloch. Other details about Henry Bloch's life and his extended family come from a series of oral interviews conducted by Matthew Reeves, Mary Ann Wynkoop, and John Herron from the University of Missouri-Kansas City. These interviews began in August of 2015 and concluded in September of 2016. Finally, additional material about Henry's life came from a series of letters written between Henry and his parents and

brothers. These letters, mostly dated from the early 1940s, are in possession of the Bloch family.

2. On the history of the University of Kansas City, see Christopher Wolff, *A Pearl of Great Value: The History of UMKC, Kansas City's University* (Kansas City: UMKC Books, 2016). On the history of the University of Michigan, see Howard H. Peckham, *The Making of the University of Michigan, 1817-1992* (Ann Arbor: The University of Michigan Press, 1994). For a brief biographical sketch about Henry Wollman, see the class notes section of the *Michigan Alumnus* (vol. 34): 1927-1928 and a second version from (vol. 42), April 11, 1936. Copies of the Michigan yearbook, *The Michiganensian*, a valuable source for this chapter, are available from the Bentley Historical Library at the University of Michigan. While in Ann Arbor, Henry wrote frequent letters to his family. These informative letters describe everything from his class schedule to his social habits and are also included in the family collection of letters made available for this project.

3. There are many sources on the history of the Eighth Air Force, but as a representative sample, consider Roger Anthony Freeman, *The Mighty Eighth: Units, Men, and Machine, A History of the US 8th Army Air Force* (New York: Doubleday, 1970); Martin Bowman, *8th Air Force at War: Memories and Missions, England 1942-1945* (Cambridge: Patrick Stephens, 1994); Ian McLachlan and Russell J. Zorn, *Eighth Air Force Bomber Stories: Eye-Witness Accounts from American Airmen and British Civilians of the Perils of War* (Yeovil, UK: Patrick Stephens, 1991); and Gerald Aster, *The Mighty Eighth: The Air War in Europe as Told by the Men Who Fought It* (New York: Berkley Caliber, 1997). The National Museum of the Mighty Eighth Air Force in Pooler, Georgia, is also an excellent source of information about this unit.

Training for War

1. Henry's frequent letters home continued after he joined the Air Corps. Descriptions of army routines and his impressions of military life at various training centers in Texas and Florida are included in these letters.

2. The Air Force Historical Research Agency, housed at Maxwell Air Force Base in Montgomery, Alabama, and open to the public, is the primary repository for all documents related to the Air Force. Much of the information in this chapter about training, bases, and war preparation comes from their materials and publications. On the nature of Army Air Corps training programs see *The Army Air Forces in World War II, Vol. 1, Plans and Early Operations: January 1939-Augsut 1942*, editors Wesley Frank Craven and James Lea Cate (Washington D.C.: Air Force Historical Studies Office, 1948). This book is a product of the Washington D.C.-based Air Force Historical Support Division sponsored by the Air Force History and Museums program. This program produced a number of informative studies about the history and operations of the Air Force during World War II. Another volume in this series, *Vol. III-Europe: Argument to V-E Day, January 1944 to May 1945* (Chicago: University of Chicago Press, 1951), was also very helpful. For more information on various training bases, see also Frederick J. Shaw, *Locating Air Force Base Sites History's Legacy* (Washington, DC: United States Air Force, 2004).

3. The B-17 aircraft has received considerable attention from scholars and air force enthusiasts alike. For more information, see Edward Jablonski, *Flying Fortress* (New York: Doubleday, 1965); Bill Yenne, *B-17 at War* (St. Paul: Zenith Imprint, 2006); and Martin W. Bowman, *Castles in the Air: The Story of the B-17 Flying Fortress Crews of the 8th Air Force* (Dulles, VA: Potomac Books, 2000). Donald L. Miller's *Masters of the*

Air: America's Bomber Boys Who Fought the Air War Against Nazi Germany (New York: Simon & Schuster, 2007) was especially helpful for this chapter. On the Norden bombsight, see Albert L. Pardini, *The Legendary Norden Bombsight* (Atglen, PA: Schiffer, 1999) and Phillip A. St. John, *Bombardiers: A History, Vol. II* (Paducah, KY: Turner, 1998)

Off to War

1. This chapter owes a very heavy debt to Robert Morris with Ian Hawkins, *The Wild Blue Yonder and Beyond: The 95th Bomb Group in War and Peace* (Washington, D.C.: Potomac Books, 2012). This book traces the history of the bomb group from inception to the modern era and was an invaluable resource for this project. See also Ian L. Hawkins, *B-17s Over Berlin: Personal Stories from the 95th Bomb Group (H)* (Washington, DC: Potomac Books, 2005).

2. Information on Henry and the rest of the crew come from oral interviews with Henry, letters from Henry to his family, as well as memoirs from the other crew members, especially the pilot Frank Psota. The Psota family made their father's scrapbook from the war available for this project. This collection included souvenirs, news clippings, photographs, and an important newspaper story on Psota's experiences during the war. See Cheryl Chojnacki, "Reflecting on an Amazing Life," *Daily Herald* (Chicago) November 11, 2003.

Missions

1. On the mission record of Henry's crew, Morris' *The Wild Blue Yonder and Beyond* was once again very helpful. Detailed information about Henry's missions and flight records came from a National Archives and Records Administration (NARA) request for military records made by David Disney.

NARA provided copies of all records from each mission, including the target, distance flown, result, and crew notes from the flight. From these flight records, it was possible to reconstruct each of the missions Henry completed. See Record Group 18, Combat Mission Reports, 95th BG (H) Mission Folders, 1943-1945, National Archives and Records Administration, Silver Springs, Maryland. See also a month-by-month history of the missions of the 95th in Charles J. Brickley, *95th Bomb Group Unit History* (Maxwell A.F.B.: Air Force Historical Research Agency, 1994). The 95th Bomb Group Memorials Foundation, a veterans association based in Tucson, Arizona, also provided information about the missions and aircraft flown by Henry's crew. Finally, key information came from oral interviews with Henry about his memories from his flight experiences.

2. For more information on the 95th, see Paul M. Andrews, *Operations Record of the 95th BG(H)* (York, PA: Design Center, 1990); Ray Bowden, *Tales to Noses Over Berlin—The Eighth Air Force Missions* (London: Design Oracle Partnership, 1995); and Eugene Fletcher, *Fletcher's Gang—A B-17 Crew in Europe, 1944-45* (Seattle: University of Washington Press, 1988). For more information on flying practices, like takeoff procedures, the combat box, and crewmember responsibilities, see Roger A. Freeman, *The Mighty Eighty War Manual* (London: Cassell Military, 2002)

Day of Days

1. The literature on D-Day is extensive. See, for example, Cornelius Ryan, *The Longest Day: The Classic Epic of D-Day* (New York: Simon & Schuster, 1994) and Stephen E. Ambrose, *D-Day: June 6, 1944: The Climactic Battle of World War II* (New York: Simon & Schuster, 1994). For more information about the D-Day briefing reports, see the Combat Mission

Reports for the 95th BG cited above from the National Archives and Records Administration.

2. *The Wild Blue Yonder*, the NARA mission records, and the interviews with Henry helped to complete the portrait of Henry's experiences on D-Day and throughout the rest of his time in the European theater.

3. The French Resistance scholarship is large but for two examples, see Peter Davies, *France and the Second World War: Occupation, Collaboration and Resistance* (London: Routledge, 2000) and Julian Jackson, *France: The Dark Years, 1940-1944* (New York: Oxford University Press, 2003).

4. For more information about Operation Frantic, see Edward T. Russell, "Leaping the Atlantic Wall: Army Air Forces Campaigns in Western Europe, 1942-1945," an online source available from the United States Air Force History and Museums Program. A different perspective on these missions comes from Mark J. Conversino, *Fighting With the Soviets: The Failure of Operation Frantic, 1944-1945* (Lawrence: University Press of Kansas, 1997).

5. Eugene Fletcher, *The Lucky Bastard Club: A B-17 in Training and in Combat, 1943-1945* (Seattle: University of Washington Press, 1992).

Harvard

1. For information about Robert A. Lovett, see the "Oral interview collection" at the Harry S. Truman Library & Museum, July 7, 1971. https://www.trumanlibrary.org/oralhist/lovett.htm

See also his obituary, Albin Krebs, "R.A. Lovett, Ex-Chief of Defense who pressed buildup in 50's, Dies," *New York*

Times, May 8, 1986. On Charles "Tex" Thornton, see Robert Sobel, *The Rise and Fall of Conglomerate Kings* (Washington, D.C.: Beard Books, 1999) and David Bird, "Charles B. Thornton Dead at 68; Was a Litton Industries Founder," *New York Times*, November 26, 1981.

2. The best work on statistical control is John A. Byrne, *The Whiz Kids: The Founding Fathers of American Business and the Legacy They Left Us* (New York: Doubleday, 1993). This chapter relies heavily on Byrne's work to reconstruct the goals and operations of statistical control. Readers interested in the extraordinary history of this project and the men who supported it are encouraged to seek out Byrne's book.

3. For more information on Harvard University during the Second World War, see Corydon Ireland, "Harvard Goes to War," *Harvard Gazette*, November 10, 2011.

4. The history of Walker Air Field comes from R. Douglas Hurt, "Naval Air Stations in Kansas During World War II," *Kansas Historical Quarterly* 43 (Autumn 1977): 351-362, and Hurt, "U.S. Army and Air Force Wings Over Kansas," *Kansas Historical Quarterly* 25 (Summer 1959): 129-157. The website, "Abandoned and Little-known Airfields," also contains historical information and photographs about Walker Air Field. http://www.airfields-freeman.com/KS/Airfields_KS_C.htm#walker

5. More information about Henry's experiences at Harvard and at Walker Air Field comes from his letters to his parents and brothers as well as oral interviews with the authors.

Business

1. This discussion of the early history of United Business Services and H&R Block relies heavily on Bloch, *Many Happy*

Returns. Interviews by the authors with Henry's son, Tom Bloch, and H&R Block Foundation President, David Miles, helped fill in additional details about the early history of the company. Interviews with Henry also provided further information about his company.

Epilogue

1. Local news coverage of the rededication of the Henry Wollman Bloch Fountain was extensive. See "Renovated Henry Bloch Fountain at Union Station rededicated," *Kansas City Star,* June 30, 2016. Kerri Stowell, "Iconic fountain in front of Union Station flowing again," *Fox4News,* June 30, 2016.